T0024817

CULTURE SMART!
LAOS

Nada Matas-Runquist

·K·U·P·E·R·A·R·D·

ISBN 978 1 85733 880 5
British Library Cataloguing in Publication Data
A CIP catalogue entry for this book is available from the British Library

First published in Great Britain
by Kuperard, an imprint of Bravo Ltd
59 Hutton Grove, London N12 8DS
Tel: +44 (0) 20 8446 2440 Fax: +44 (0) 20 8446 2441
www.culturesmart.co.uk
Inquiries: sales@kuperard.co.uk

Series Editor Geoffrey Chesler
Design Bobby Birchall

Printed in India

About the Author

NADA MATAS-RUNQUIST, D.Phil., is a Croatian-born French academic, interpreter, professor, consultant, and international project manager who speaks six languages fluently and has studied three more. A true polymath, she has worked in languages, science, bioethics, law, cultural studies, and civic education. Her doctorate is from Oxford University and she has degrees from the Universities of Zagreb, Stockholm, and Otago. She has a permanent position as associate professor in multidisciplinary studies at the University of Avignon, France, and has been a guest lecturer at the University of Stanford, Shaanxi Normal University in China, and IB schools in Asia and Europe. She has studied and held academic posts in nine different countries, including the National University of Laos, and currently divides her time between Vientiane and Avignon.

The Culture Smart! series is continuing to expand. All Culture Smart! guides are available as e-books, and many as audio books. For the latest titles visit

www.culturesmart.co.uk

The publishers would like to thank **CultureSmart!**Consulting for its help in researching and developing the concept for this series.

CultureSmart!Consulting creates tailor-made seminars and consultancy programs to meet a wide range of corporate, public-sector, and individual needs. Whether delivering courses on multicultural team building in the USA, preparing Chinese engineers for a posting in Europe, training call-center staff in India, or raising the awareness of police forces to the needs of diverse ethnic communities, it provides essential, practical, and powerful skills worldwide to an increasingly international workforce.

For details, visit www.culturesmartconsulting.com

CultureSmart!Consulting and **CultureSmart!** guides have both contributed to and featured regularly in the weekly travel program "Fast Track" on BBC World TV.

contents

contents

Note: English transliteration is widely used in this guide, but you will notice a combination of different versions of English transliteration interspersed with French, all of which are currently used in Laos. This is due to the lack of consistent spelling rules for converting Lao into Latin script. For example, the capital city Vientiane can also be spelled Vieng Chan or Vien Tiane. Luang Prabang can be Luang Phrabang, or even Luang Phra Bang or Pha Bang. It can be challenging, to say the least!

Map of Laos

introduction

Once known as "The Kingdom of a Million Elephants and the White Parasol," Laos is a landlocked country of great contrast and beauty in the heart of the Indochinese Peninsula. Dominated by the mighty Mekong River, it has dense forests, mountain peaks that soar above the morning mist, and a fascinating combination of glorious Asian temples and iconic French colonial architecture. The jewel in its crown is the ancient royal capital, Luang Prabang, a UNESCO world heritage site with a stunning fusion of traditional architecture and natural landmarks.

This multiethnic land of peaceable, good-natured, and stoical people is attracting more and more enthusiastic visitors each year. Officially Laos is a one-party socialist republic, governed by the Lao People's Revolutionary Party, but it has ambitious industrial development strategies, is opening up to foreign investment, and today is a member of ASEAN and the WTO. Its capital, Vientiane, is catching up fast with other dynamic Asian cities, with Thailand, a stone's throw across the Mekong, providing both inspiration and commercial stimulus.

It is easy to lose oneself in Laos' exotic and lush environment, where there is also a remarkable sense of stepping back in time. Visitors quickly relax and enjoy the vibrancy and color of the bustling marketplaces with their aromatic spices, tropical fruits, and huge wicker baskets containing many varieties of rice. You may glimpse a group of monks of all ages wandering past in flowing orange robes, and later hear their chanting from within the temple walls. Passing a line of laughing and chattering children in school uniform, you will always be greeted with gracious bows and the traditional salutation, "*Sabaidee.*"

Culture Smart! Laos aims to take you one step further. It provides essential cultural information, including a brief historical overview for context and insights and advice on local customs and lifestyles. Despite the official Marxism-Leninism of the government, Buddhist culture and traditional Asian values pervade every aspect of life in Laos. The overwhelming majority of the population lives in small villages in rural areas, until recently far removed from the intrusion of the state or the material blandishments and economic pressures of the outside world. On an individual level Lao people tend to seek consensus and avoid confrontation, and are remarkably accepting of the vicissitudes of life. Order and harmony have traditionally been cardinal values. Despite the harsh living conditions of many, they're genuinely friendly, kind, humble, and very curious about foreigners— though sometimes comments made in good humor may strike Westerners as a bit personal. Respect and deference are shown to elders, social superiors, and those in authority.

The information here, collected through research and the experience of living and working in Laos, will also be of great use to businessmen and prospective investors. Whatever the purpose of your visit, you will be greeted with warmth, courtesy, and hospitality, and feel completely safe in this beautiful country.

Bon voyage to Laos!

Key Facts

Official Name	Lao PDR (Lao People's Democratic Republic). In Lao: SPP Lao (Sathalanalat Paxathipathai Paxaxon Lao)	The Lao refer to their own country as Pathet Lao, which means "Lao Country."
Population	Approx. 7,000,000	More than 70 percent of the population live in small villages (averaging about 300 inhabitants).
Capital City	Vientiane	Pop. 200–600,000, depending on definition of town area
Main Cities	Pakse (pop. 88,000), Thakhek (85,000), Savannakhet (66,000), Luang Prabang (47,000)	Luang Prabang is the ancient royal city and a UNESCO World Heritage Site.
Area	91,875 square miles (237,955 sq. km)	The highest mountain is Phou Bia (9,249 ft/2,819 m).
Borders	Myanmar (Burma) and China to the northwest, Vietnam to the east, Cambodia to the south, and Thailand to the west and southwest	
Climate	Tropical, typical wet–dry season of the region. Rarely windy, being far from any sea	

Currency	The Lao Kip. Code: LAK	US dollars and Thai baht are widely accepted in Vientiane.
Ethnic Makeup	More than 100 ethnic groups, 49 officially recognized ethnic groups	
Languages	Lao is the official language, spoken by roughly half of the population.	Laos is highly multilingual; there are an estimated 80 recognized living languages and around 120 distinct dialects in the country
Religion	No official state religion	The most emblematic Buddhist shrine features on the national emblem.
Government	Communist. One-party state with a unicameral parliament, the 149-member National Assembly	
Electricity	230 volts, 50 Hz	Both US and EU plugs. Bring adaptors.
Internet Domain	.la	
Telephone	The Laos county code is 856.	To dial abroad out of Laos, dial 00.
Time Zone	(Laos) Standard Time is 7 hours ahead of Greenwich Mean Time (GMT +7)	Laos does not operate daylight saving time.

LAND &
PEOPLE

Until just a few years ago Laos was isolated and
frozen in time as one of the world's last communist
states. Bordered by Myanmar (Burma) and China to
the northwest, Vietnam to the east, Cambodia to the
south, and Thailand to the west and southwest, it
remains one of Asia's poorest and most underdeveloped countries.

Laos has a fascinating multiethnic mix of people
and heritage and, for diverse reasons, although war
has played a major role more than once, is only now
opening up to the world. Since the collapse of the
Soviet Union in 1991, the Lao People's Democratic
Republic (Lao PDR) has struggled to establish its
position and identity within an ever-changing and
challenging political and economic context.

Some Laotians born during the Indochina Wars
have never known their date of birth. There were
no official records, and everyone was caught up in
the tragedy of war and violence. Today, the United
Nations' Sustainable Development Goals (SDGs)
are of the utmost importance in Lao PDR. The UN's
SDG18 has the specific objective of reducing the
impact of unexploded ordnance (UXO) that is still
in the ground from that terrible period.

Laos and its people are now experiencing the
impact of foreign enterprise and massive investment
in tourism, rail links, and hydropower. With

economic and social progress, many fear that essential traditional values are in danger of being lost.

GEOGRAPHY

Laos is smaller in area than the United Kingdom. It has a total boundary length of 3,158 miles (5,083 km) and is dominated by the Mekong River. Its capital is Vientiane, established in 1563. Approximately 80 percent of the country is hilly or mountainous, with many remote and inaccessible areas. The remaining 20 percent is lowland, where more than half the country's population live.

A huge range of limestone mountains lie to the north, with peaks as high as 8,200 feet (2,500 m). The Bolaven Plateau in the south is home to coffee plantations, and the flat rice fields stretching from the southeast to the northwest are rendered fertile by the Mekong River. However, the diversity of landscape

is rapidly diminishing in the face of major agrarian transformation, in which large, monoculture plantations are changing both the physical setting and the daily lives of people. Only 25 percent of the country's land area is considered cultivable. Despite the fact that just over 70 percent of the total cultivated area is still dedicated to rice, Laos relies heavily on food imports from neighboring countries.

The country is geographically varied and beautiful, from high, mist-capped mountains to grassy plains, plateaus, dense forest, and paddy fields flanking the Mekong. Its people are gentle and welcoming.

CLIMATE

Laos has the typical wet–dry season of the region, with the wet season ranging from April/May to September/October. The best time for a visit is considered to be during the dry season, as the weather isn't too hot; however it tends to be busier then, and even during the rainy season the rain is not generally heavy for long periods.

Because Laos is far from any sea it is rarely windy, as the mountains on the east block the wind coming from the coast of Vietnam, which means that it gets very hot during the monsoon months, especially in low-lying Vientiane. On the plateaus and mountains, the weather is milder, and it can be really cold in winter. There is a great contrast between day and night temperatures, and warm clothing is essential.

During the months preceding the monsoon, the dry, fertile areas along the river banks are planted and, with the arrival of the rainy season, the rivers completely flood again and this cherished water revitalizes the soil for growth.

Life in Laos is still essentially based on seasonal tasks to be completed from dawn to dusk. Despite the standing joke about there being only two seasons in Laos—hot and hotter—winter does exist in all parts of the country, and lasts several weeks. Around the time of the Western New Year, night temperatures can drop as low as 50°F (10°C), even catching people out in Vientiane and elsewhere by the Mekong River. During this cold snap, people rarely go out after nightfall, food stalls are not open, and entertaining is based in homes, with large servings of warm soup for everyone, or small fires laid outside for all to sit round. Temperatures are much more extreme in the mountains, with winters lasting considerably longer and people ensuring that they are home before dark.

THE ENVIRONMENT

Laos is tropical and mountainous, with many limestone formations and dry, tall, hardwood dipterocarp forests. There is not a great deal of primary forest left, as there is a lot of illegal Siamese rosewood logging and conservation laws are not administered efficiently. Protected forests are not heavily guarded, and trees are felled to supply the manufacture of massive wooden furniture. The only effective deterrent for poachers is UXOs (Unexploded Ordnance).

Laos has a reputation for its beautiful and unspoiled environment. Tourism and the impact of economic and industrial progress, however, are changing the ecological balance. It is still sometimes called "the Land of a Million Elephants," but this is no longer the case, and the magnificent Asian elephant *Elephas maximus*, once used for heavy work in the logging industry, has become an endangered species.

What used to be the country's largest nature park, Nam Theun, on the Nakai Plateau, was flooded by a dam to create two hydropower projects. NT2 is the largest hydroelectric project so far in Laos.

Flora and Fauna
Northern Laos has tropical rainforests with broad-leaved evergreens, while in the south there are monsoon forests with a combination of evergreens and deciduous trees, where the ground is covered with tall, coarse grass, wild banana, and bamboo. There is a stunning variety of orchids and palms.

Look out for the cannonball tree *Couroupita guianensis*, an amazing tropical tree of religious significance in India. These trees have beautiful, fragrant flowers and large, round fruits that bang loudly when they drop off—hence their common name! You can still find them by temples that have become part of urban areas over the years, such as Wat Si Muang in Vientiane.

Laos is home to nearly 200 varieties of mammals and more than 700 species of birds. Monkeys, rats, and deer dominate the mammalian part of the jungle fauna, elephants, rhinoceroses, tigers, and leopards being some of the most endangered species in Laos. Gibbons and the snub-nosed langur are endemic. Exotic animals are usually found in greater numbers in Laos than in neighboring countries because there is more forest and the human population is smaller. They include the leopard, tiger, Asiatic black bear, and even the Javan mongoose. The endangered freshwater Irrawaddy dolphin lives in the Mekong River on the Lao and Cambodian border, easily observed from boats (for hire on Don Khon island).

There are countless varieties of insects, frogs, lizards, snakes, and other reptiles. Many water birds live in the lowlands of the Mekong, with other birds, such as parrots and songbirds, keeping to the jungles.

The Mighty Mekong
The Mekong, also known in Lao as the Mae Nam Khong, is the world's twelfth-longest river, flowing 2,700 miles (4,350 km) through the heart of Southeast Asia. The river's source is on the Tibetan Plateau, and it runs through China, Myanmar, Laos, Thailand, Cambodia, and Vietnam. The Mekong has extraordinary biodiversity and is difficult to navigate because there are extreme seasonal variations in flow, and many rapids, waterfalls, and dams. In the rainy season, enormous amounts of natural debris, such as tree trunks, make navigation and even swimming dangerous. Only local village children swim in the river. The mythical water snake known as the *naga* originates in the Mekong, and its image features often in Laos, from woven textiles to temples, and many businesses have it in their name.

The Mekong Basin boasts the richest area of biodiversity in the world after the Amazon. Estimates include about 20,000 plant species, 430 mammals, 1,200 birds, 800 reptiles, and 850 fish species; 87 percent of the fish species are migratory. It is home to more giant fish than any other river on Earth.

River transportation and fish migration are frequently impeded by the construction of dams, on the Mekong itself or its tributaries. There are currently more than fifteen hydropower projects in Laos that use dams to store or divert water for electricity generation. This is not without controversy as, although the dams are promoted as a vital source of economic growth, the flooding and water diversions are affecting both the environment and long-standing local industries. To allow the free migration of fish, "fish ladders" or "elevators" have been constructed alongside the dams; these are a series of watery shelves that allow migrating species to make their way upstream unimpeded by obstacles. However, this measure is not fully effective; for example, the protected Mekong catfish is endangered through lack of the deep water it needs for migration. The Mekong River Commission manages the river for commercial purposes, but there are no conservation laws in place. Six huge bridges span it at various points.

The riverfront in Vientiane has changed completely in the last decade. A few charming local restaurants clinging to the sandbanks remain, but now there is a concrete esplanade (built also to protect the city from flooding), complete with jogging paths and exercise machines. Gradually, the traditional unspoiled charm in the cities and urban areas close to the river is being replaced with a skyline of more and more high-rise buildings and numerous electricity pylons.

THE PEOPLE

Although this region of Asia is home to more than half of humanity, the population of Laos is small—only 2 million in 1960, though it has now reached 7 million. It has the youngest population of any country in Asia, with a median age of 21.6 years. The population is very unevenly spread, with most people living in the valleys of the Mekong River and its tributaries.

Life expectancy has grown from 54 in 2007 to 60 for men and 65 for women in 2016, as more people gain access to clean water and health care. According to NAFRI (National Agriculture and Forestry Research Institute), more than 70 percent of the population live in small villages, averaging about 300 inhabitants, in rural areas.

One probably unique situation is that, while there are 7 million Lao in Lao PDR, there is a closely linked ethnic Lao population living across the Mekong River in an area of Thailand called Issan (also spelled Isan or Isarn) that is three times larger than the population of Laos itself. These people are sometimes referred to as

Issan Lao, Thai Issan, Thai-Lao, or Lao-Issan. This situation stems from the Franco–Siamese Treaty of 1907 that formalized the Lao border with Thailand.

The Main Ethnic Groups

There are forty-nine officially recognized ethnic groups in the country, but many sources mention up to or more than a hundred. Each preserves its own language or dialect, local customs, culture, and ancient traditions. Lao Loum, or lower-land Lao, form more than half of the population, and at 65 percent are thus the predominant group. The second largest group, Lao Theung, accounts for 22 percent of the population. Lao Soung, which includes the Hmong and the Yao, account for 9 percent. The remainder of the inhabitants have settled from neighboring countries. (2015 census.)

There are strict customary codes of behavior, but livelihoods are similar, with most groups practicing slash and burn agriculture, and in the past some cultivated opium as a cash crop. Ethnic groups tend

to stick together and live in homogeneous communities, but other groups do coexist with them, with the inevitable intermarrying and overlapping of culture and religion. Populations from different ethnicities were thrown together during mandatory military service before and after 1975. Globalization and modern trends, however, are endangering this unique social structure.

President Obama—the first North American president to set foot on Laos soil—was particularly thoughtful during his visit in 2016, when he addressed this diverse, multiethnic nation as "the people of Laos," and complimented them on a richness of culture that has hitherto passed many by. The term "Laotians," to indicate all the people of Laos, is mainly used in the French language, and in refugee communities overseas, but is rarely used in English within Laos.

LAO AMERICANS, LAO FRENCH ...

Many people from Laos who were forced, or chose, to leave the country, generally fall into these categories. They are also known as overseas Lao, American, and French Lao, or Laotians.

The émigré Lao struggled hard to rebuild their lives, often passing through refugee camps before moving to a new country. To this day, and even though they have taken on American and French or other nationality, many have held on to their Lao heritage, worshiping in their temples, honoring their elders, dancing the *lamvong*, and so on.

Why did so many Laotians become American, Canadian, or French, knowing that there are Lao refugee communities in many other countries— Australia, New Zealand, UK, Japan, French Guiana? A great number of survivors of the Hmong "secret army" fled the country during the Communist regime, and so too did the country's academics and professional elite. Both France and the US were involved in wars in Laos, and the Hmong in particular fought alongside the French in the battle of Dien Bien Phu and then the Americans in the Secret War. Thus a subsequent "debt" owed to these people facilitated emigration, and approximately 100,000 moved to the USA.

Other Lao sought refugee status in France. Many followed the French OMI priest Father Yves Bertrais to French Guiana, an overseas department of France in South America, where the French encouraged resettlement of whole communities. Here, the Hmong have dominated fruit and vegetable production since their arrival, with many people unaware of their origin and considering them to be a local tribe. French Guiana, in fact, became home to many multiethnic tribes.

Some Lao then moved from Guiana to France. These remarkable people, who arrived empty-handed in a foreign land (albeit similar to theirs in climate), speaking a language that was never recorded in written form, were granted French nationality and gradually adapted to their new surroundings. Their children became literate in the French language, and now some do not know their forebears' native tongue. More ambitious students have been able to pursue university degrees in France and build their lives there, although exotic Guiana with Lao heritage remains "home."

Some Lao moved to other countries, including Canada and Australia.

A BRIEF HISTORY

One of the difficulties of recounting the history of Laos is the sheer lack of records. Even if there are archaeological findings, palm-leaf manuscripts, records from neighboring countries, and colonial records, there is still very little information available from reliable written sources. Laos was an isolated landlocked country for so long, barely known to the world. Many of its people were illiterate, and their history was only related orally. The effect of globalization has not necessarily helped to enlighten anyone about Laos either—if anything, it has opened up a plethora of inaccurate "facts" posted on the Internet and, with the gradual loss of oral tradition among the ethnic tribes, many people in Laos may never know their history. There is not even a consensus on the date of independence from France—1949, 1953 (the most used), 1954?

Laos has experienced many transitions, ranging from the early dynastic rule to French colonial administration to royal nationalism and, finally, revolutionary socialism. Its geopolitical strength lay in certain extraordinary natural features such as the amazing Khone Waterfall, the largest in Southeast Asia, which acted as a barrier against invaders penetrating Laos by river, and the enormous and life-giving Mekong River. Nevertheless, over the past two centuries, the area under Lao political control has progressively contracted due to the external influences of different countries.

Early Times
There is archaeological evidence of communities living in Laos as early as 3000 BCE, with remains of pottery and metal objects that prove that they worked the land. From the eighth to the second centuries CE an inland trading society emerged in the north, around the megalithic site called the Plain of Jars. The mysterious jars may or may not be sarcophagi

from the Iron Age (500 BCE–800 CE). According to
tradition, the area of Lan Xang was first mentioned
in late 700 CE by local king Thoa Khun, who fought
intermittently with the Thai, Burmese, Vietnamese,
and Khmer.

From a Province of the Khmer Empire to the Lan Xang Kingdom

The area of Laos was a province of the Khmer Empire
for about four centuries before being united for
the first time in 1353. Recorded history exists only
from the fourteenth century—prior to that only
myths and legends shape our knowledge. It was at
this point that Laos' history was first recorded by
the great warrior Fa Ngum, who conquered many
territories and founded the Lan Xang kingdom. Here
he developed an effective administrative system, an
elaborate military organization, and conducted active

commerce with neighboring countries.

Fa Ngum, helped by the Angkor Khmer sovereign, is known to have extended the Khmer civilization, which was already "Indianized," in the upper Mekong River. He also introduced Theravada Buddhism, through Khmer missionaries from Angkor.

In 1373 Fa Ngum was succeeded by his son, Oun Heuan, better known as Sam Sen Thai. He followed his father's efficient guidelines, and all was well until the Vietnamese invaded, starting a period of wars with neighbors. This period, from the mid-1500s, brought about two centuries of conflict with Burma as well as the Thai kingdom of Phra Nakhon Si Ayutthaya (also called and spelled as Ayutthaya, Ayudhya, Ayuthia, or Ayuthaya, and now a UNESCO World Heritage site).

Lan Xang achieved its greatest territorial expansion under King Photisarath, who was a devout Buddhist. His son, Setthathirath, first acquired the throne of the northern Thai state of Chiang Mai (Chiengmai, or Lanna) before ascending to the throne of Lan Xang. It was King Setthathirath who transferred the Laotian capital from Luang Prabang to Vientiane in 1560 and embarked on an extensive building program. However, a few years after his death Myanmar seized Vientiane (1574) and ravaged the country, which lapsed into anarchy until Souligna Vongsa ascended the throne in 1637 and restored order.

The Golden Age and the Division of the Kingdom

Souligna Vongsa (1613–94) was the king of Lan Xang during its period of greatest prosperity, and the first to see European explorers arriving in Laos. He was a patron of the arts and staunch defender of Buddhism, introducing Buddhist education to the new capital, and establishing what is considered to be the "Golden Age" of Laos. He died in 1685 without an heir.

In 1707, internal conflicts resulted in the split of Lan Xang into two kingdoms: Luang Prabang in the north (present-day upper Laos) and Vientiane in the south (lower Laos). Strong neighboring states took advantage of this split to invade the region. Vientiane was overrun and annexed by Siam (Thailand) in 1828, while Luang Prabang became a vassal state of both the Chinese and the Vietnamese.

Indochina vs French Indochina

The term Indochina is considered more geographical than political, although it has had a historical and cultural impact. These days it refers to the continental portion of the region now known as Southeast Asia, covering present-day Vietnam, Laos, Thailand, Cambodia, and Myanmar, as well as (sometimes) the Malaysian Peninsula and even Singapore.

The term was later adopted as the name of the colony of French Indochina, covering only three of these countries—Vietnam, Laos, and Cambodia— hile the whole area of historic Indochina might now be referred to as the Indochinese Peninsula.

The French Period

Laos was made part of French Indochina at the very end of the nineteenth century, and gained independence in 1953. In 1893 France, which had already established a protectorate over what is now central and northern Vietnam, extended its control to both Vientiane and Luang Prabang. Laos thus became part of the Union of Indochina under the overall authority of a governor-general based in Hanoi—together with Tonking (Tongkin, Tonquin, or Tongking, or northern Vietnam); Annam (central Vietnam); and Cochinchina (southern Vietnam, around the Mekong Delta), three regions that make today's Vietnam, as well as Cambodia.

France administered Laos as a unified territory from 1899/1900. However, the northern half of Laos was technically a protectorate and the southern half was a colony. It was not until 1941 that the kingdom of Luang Prabang became the kingdom of Laos.

During the Second World War the French colonial authorities, as servants of the French Vichy government, remained in place. After the fall of Vichy toward the end of the war in Europe, the Japanese assumed control, until Japan itself surrendered and the French returned. The war period saw a great decline in French prestige.

The First Indochina War (1946–54)

This conflict is also known as the French Indochina War. In 1945 the Vietnamese nationalist leader Ho Chi Minh, who had spent part of his life in France, proclaimed the independence of Vietnam. The French opposed independence, and Ho Chi Minh led a guerrilla war against them, which concluded with Vietnamese victory at Dien Bien Phu, about ten miles (15 km) from the Lao border. General Henri Navarre was then the French military commander. The majority of the fighting was located in Tonkin in the north of Vietnam, but the war affected the whole country, extending into neigboring Laos and Cambodia.

The Lao Issara Movement

Free Laos, "Lao Issara," was founded in 1945 as a political movement against French colonial rule. The departure of the Japanese from Laos in 1945 left the Laotian ruling elite divided over the issue of the restoration of French control. The granting of limited independence within the French union in 1949 split the Lao Issara: one faction returned from exile to join the royalist government, which enjoyed semi-autonomy as an "associated state" within the French Union; the other faction of the Lao Issara allied with the north Vietnamese and formed the Pathet Lao.

The Geneva Conference

In July 1954 the Geneva Conference agreement, which officially ended the First Indochina War, declared Laos to be a unified independent kingdom, but the deeply divided country continued to be torn apart by three factions (see below). It left neighboring Vietnam divided roughly in half, between the communist North and the non-communist South. The scarcely populated northeastern provinces then became a regrouping area for pro-communist Pathet Lao guerrillas. Cambodia was left territorially intact. American policy and the imperatives of the Cold War meant that all three non-communist governments were fully expected to play their part in containing the spread of communism.

The Political Battle for Control Between the "Three Lao Princes"

The Lao monarchy, which dates back to the 1300s, shared power with the communist Pathet Lao on and off through the 1960s and '70s. Many of the members of the royal family went to study and live in France.

The political battle for control over Laos was between the "Three Lao Princes"—Prince Souvanna Phouma, his half-brother Souphanouvong, and Boun Oum Na Champassak from the southern Kingdom of Champasak. All three are still considered by some to be the most important political leaders of post-colonial Laos, but with radically different political views. Prince Souvanna Phouma was considered a pragmatic prime minister who did his best to bring the competing factions together. His neutral position was supported by US President John F. Kennedy and the Geneva Conference of 1961. Souphanouvong was called the "Red Prince," because of his full support of the socialist revolutionaries, and then there was the conservative Prince Boun Oum, who totally opposed communism. Backed by the Soviet Union and the North Vietnamese Army, the communist Pathet Lao forces overthrew the royalist government in 1975.

The Second Indochina War (1954–75)

More commonly known as the "Vietnam War," this is also called the "American War" in Vietnam (in full, the "War Against the Americans to Save the Nation"). This war was also part of a larger regional conflict and a manifestation of the Cold War between the United States and the Soviet Union and their respective allies.

The main conflict was based on North Vietnam's intent to unify the country under a single communist regime modeled on those of the Soviet Union and China, having defeated the French colonial administration of Vietnam in 1954.

North Vietnam was supported by Soviet, Chinese, and Eastern Bloc allies, and was fighting against South Vietnam and the United States and their allies from South Korea, Thailand, and even Australia and New Zealand. Some of the most critical battles took place in the remote northeastern mountainous areas of Laos inhabited by hill tribes. Many of the indigenous Hmong opted to join the anti-communist forces in order to eject North Vietnam from Laos, and some of the Khmu and Mien ethnic groups joined in. In Laos the First and Second Indochina wars (1946–75) are referred to as the Thirty Year Struggle.

Communist Takeover with Prince as President
With the ending of the war in Vietnam, the Pathet Lao, renamed the Lao People's Front, seized power and declared Laos a democratic republic on December 2, 1975, with the Lao People's Revolutionary Party (LPRP, founded in 1955 and called the Lao People's Party until 1972) as the only legal political party. Their world view shared a revolutionary outlook with Vietnam. The Lao leaders had a long and close relationship with their Vietnamese communist allies. Before founding the Party, they had been members of the Indochina Communist Party. Most spoke Vietnamese, and some had family ties with Vietnam: the Party's general secretary, Kaysone Phomvihan, had a Vietnamese father; and the second in rank Nouhak Phoumsavan and Prince Souphanouvong had Vietnamese wives.

The 600-year-old monarchy was thus abolished and King Savang Vatthana, who had inherited the throne from his father in 1959 but was never officially crowned, was forced to abdicate and later sent to a "reeducation camp." Kaysone Phomvihane became prime minister and Prince Souphanouvong was then sworn in as president.

Concern About Laos

The Geneva Conference of 1954 had divided Vietnam at the 17th parallel, and confirmed the status of Laos as an independent state, to be ruled by the royal Lao government from Vientiane. In response, members of the pro-communist Pathet Lao regrouped in the northern provinces of Sam Neua and Phong Saly. The French were allowed to maintain a small military presence in the country to train the Royal Lao Army.

The official CIA accounts indicate that Laotian independence met US policy requirements as long as the government remained non-communist. Laos represented one of the dominoes in Southeast Asia that concerned the USA. Although the country had little intrinsic value to the West, its geographical position placed it in the center of the Cold War in Southeast Asia. If Laos fell to the Communists, Thailand could be next, according to the domino theory. And the collapse of Thailand would lead to communist domination of Southeast Asia, and perhaps beyond.

The Secret War

America's secret and silent war in Laos is still the largest paramilitary operation ever undertaken, as defined by the CIA itself. Air America, a civil airline secretly owned by the CIA, was a vital component in the Agency's operations in Laos. This is still both a delicate and controversial issue, but is now recognized as a tragic event in Laos thanks to this speech by US President Obama, given during his official visit as president in 2016: "Over nine years—from 1964 to 1973—the United States dropped more than two million tons of bombs here in Laos—more than we dropped on Germany and Japan combined during all of World War II. It made Laos, per person, the most heavily bombed country in history. As one Laotian said, the 'bombs fell like rain.' Villages and entire valleys were obliterated. The ancient Plain of Jars was devastated. Countless civilians were killed. And that conflict was another reminder that, whatever the cause, whatever our intentions, war inflicts a terrible toll, especially on innocent men, women and children. I stand with you in acknowledging the suffering and sacrifices on all sides of that conflict."

This massive bombardment was certainly not a secret for everyone. America's involvement was well known in Vientiane, and partially covered in the international press. Eventually it became well publicized and was even investigated by Congress. But the "secret" label stuck to America's war in Laos, in part because of official denials and in part because of public indifference.

The communist takeover followed: in Cambodia (by the Khmer Rouge) and South Vietnam (by the Viet Cong) in April 1975, and then in Laos (by the Pathet Lao) in December 1975.

The French Legacy
When it was a French protectorate, Laos had a very small population (470,000 inhabitants in 1900), and was very much looked on as the poor neighbor within Indochina. Within the Indochinese Union, French was the common language of civil servants and the first foreign language in schools, and this legacy is still evident. A small Lao elite, recruited from no more than 200 families throughout the country and mainly living around Luang Prabang, Vientiane, Pakse, and a few other urban areas, was distinguished by its use of the French language and the assimilation of French culture.

Only about six miles (10 km) of railroad tracks were laid by the French during that time, which illustrates their overall lack of economic interest in the country.

UXO and Metal Remains From the War

Laos has the unenviable status of being the country most affected by cluster munitions in the world. The term UXO is used generically for both unexploded ordnance (UXO) and abandoned explosive ordnance (AXO). Over the years, canny locals have used much of the metal from retrieved ordnance for scrap and recycling purposes, making some a tidy profit. Such metals have also been reworked as jewelry, decorative ornaments, pots, knives, tools, and even parts for fencing and building structures. Visitors are advised to refrain from buying UXO souvenirs, to discourage the trade in an effort to keep people safe from the dangers of UXO.

UXO incidents are still a major problem in some regions, notably the Plain of Jars and in rural areas along Laos' border with Vietnam, and people are warned to stay strictly within the white marked areas that indicate a safe path. Gun collections have been periodically undertaken since that time, too, greatly reducing the number held by civilians.

Many of the cluster bombs that were dropped have never exploded. More than forty years after the end of the war, UXO still affects approximately 25 percent of villages in fifteen of the nation's eighteen provinces. The Xieng Khouang region was one of the most heavily bombed areas, along with the southern provinces of Laos, which formed part of the Ho Chi Minh trail and which were carpet-bombed to prevent supplies being taken into Vietnam during the war. The evidence of the bombing is very clear when flying over certain areas of Laos, with visible craters pitting the land, particularly in the province of Xieng Khouang. Some have eventually become ponds.

FLAGS AND EMBLEMS

The history of the Lao flag goes back to 1953, when the royal government and the Pathet Lao struggled for political power, and the Pathet Lao succeeded by allying itself with the royal government first before taking over. At this time the royalist government used a red flag with the royalist insignia of a three-headed elephant and a ceremonial umbrella. The Pathet Lao flag design was blue with red stripes at the top and bottom and a white disk in the center. This became the national flag of the Lao People's Democratic Republic in 1975 when the monarch was deposed, with the red stripes symbolizing the blood shed by the people in order to achieve freedom, and the color blue the Mekong River, as well as representing prosperity and wealth for the people. Curiously, this is the only communist country today that does not feature a five-pointed star in its flag.

The national flag resembles the Thai flag, but it also contains the white disk symbolizing the full moon. According to the *Encyclopedia Britannica*, the white disk honored the Japanese who had promoted the Lao independence movement in the Second World War, and also symbolizes a bright future for the country.

The fragrant *dok champa* flower *Plumeria rubra*, or frangipani, is Laos' national flower.

The Kingdom of Lan Xang vs Lao PDR

The original title of Laos, "The Kingdom of a Million Elephants and the White Parasol," was based on the traditional symbols of the Lao people. The mythical first ruler of Laos, King Fa Ngum, had arrived riding a white elephant, an animal held in great reverence by the peoples of Southeast Asia, while the parasol, or royal umbrella, has long served as an important part of the king's ceremonial regalia. The white three-headed elephant and white parasol on a red field was chosen by the kingdom of Luang Prabang, which became a French protectorate in 1893, and, on May 11, 1947, by the kingdom of Laos.

Hammer and Sickle vs That Luang

Today, the national emblem is defined in the Laos constitution, and the present version was adapted to reflect the political changes on the international scene in 1991. The alteration reflects the importance of the country's national shrine, Pha That Luang, whose golden stupa replaces the previous image of the red star and hammer and sickle in the upper section that clearly signified a communist state. However, Laos is one of the few countries still under communist rule. The fact that this iconic Buddhist shrine now features on the constitutionally recognized national symbol can be interpreted as illustrating the cultural rather than the religious value of Buddhism as perceived by the current ruling party.

THE URBAN–RURAL DIVIDE

Laos has a relatively low standard of living, and until recently nearly 70 percent of the population worked in agriculture, fisheries, and forestry, living in rural and riverside areas. However, there are growing concerns about the sustainability of crops and fish stocks due to several factors, such as the growth of different industries on a large scale, an increasing population, a change in weather patterns, and resettlement. This means that the urban–rural divide is now changing. Farmers have had to move away from land that they could no longer benefit from, having exhausted attempts such as cash cropping in order to survive, and which have also diminished the soil quality. Both they, and many fishermen, have been resettled to make way for various ambitious projects promoted for theoretical economic advantages. They may have sought rural work farther afield or, in the case of young people, aspired to what they perceived to be a better life in urban areas, with access to better education and non-agricultural jobs.

Therefore, gone are some of the picturesque scenes as described by the French explorers Garnier and Pavie in the Mekong expeditions of the late 1800s, with clusters of houses along the river under swaying palm trees and the women doing their washing on the banks, able to catch fresh fish and gather rice from the paddies close by. Nowadays, many people live in houses built on the roadside, with electric cables and satellite dishes, and the occupants have little paid work of any kind. It is, of course, still possible to experience the authenticity and charm of many riverside villages.

After the Soviet regime collapsed in the early 1990s and Russia drew back from playing a key role in Laos, other countries became involved on different levels. Sweden set up a development office in 1977 to support the forestry, road, and health sectors, followed by various other cooperation projects, and then completely withdrew from the country in 2007. The US, Australia, and Japan also came in, and eventually China. They were, and still are, also interested in investing in Laos.

GOVERNMENT TODAY
Laos is a one-party state with a unicameral parliament, the 149-member National Assembly (Sapha Heng Xat).

The current assembly was elected in 2016 for a five-year term. In addition, the Lao People's Revolutionary Party (LPRP), the ruling Communist Party, holds its Congress every five years. It appoints a Central Committee and a Politburo. The prime minister (who is a member of the Politburo and Central Committee, but not the National Assembly) leads the administration of eighteen ministries and three ministry-equivalent bodies. Laos' eighteen provinces are administered by provincial governors. Districts are administered by district governors, and villages—the lowest level of the official administrative structure—are administered by village chiefs who lead village committees. Most ministries also have offices at provincial and district level.

THE ECONOMY
Poor and landlocked, and still under a communist regime backed by China and Vietnam, Laos began opening up to capitalist investment at the end of the 1980s. In 1997 it became a member of ASEAN (The Association of Southeast Asian Nations), which enabled it to participate in joint ventures with other countries in

the region, and to offer foreign investors an established economic framework. It joined the WTO in 2013. Regional collaboration was further formalized by the establishment in 2015 of AEC (the ASEAN Economic Community) to enable a free flow of goods, services, labor, investment, and capital among the member states.

In the last decade, GDP in Laos averaged 7.8 per cent, mainly attributable to the exploitation of natural resources such as water, minerals, and forests. Economic growth in 2017 was slower, due to a slight drop in investment and tourism, but this was compensated for by more agriculture, providing jobs for Lao workers.

The local economy consists of small family businesses such as retail, handicrafts, and personal services, which operate from people's homes or close by. Major difficulties are caused by a lack of skills in the face of fiercely competitive neighboring markets, along with limited institutional support, resources, logistics, finance, and simple know-how. The government recognizes the importance of family businesses, which clearly create job opportunities and boost household incomes, and encourages the community to make good use of their talents and resources. It also encourages training and collaboration with the private sector in the country, and with key international organizations.

Laos currently falls into the category of LDCs (Least Developed Countries). While the government had hoped to graduate from that status by 2020, the earliest date for possible graduation is now 2024. It is already considered by its neighbors to be a country of huge potential growth and business opportunities, where, in addition, there is plenty of land and a relatively small population. Many Web sites and advertisements now promote investment in Laos, describing it as one of the fastest-growing countries in ASEAN.

Laos has signed trade agreements with several countries, and there are two major and probably life-changing projects on track. The first is the nearly 500-mile (800-km) railway line running through the mountains from China's Yunnan Province through Vientiane to the Thai port of Rayong. Scheduled for completion by 2020, the joint venture operates on a government-to-government basis, with special incentives such as commercial developments close to the stations to attract commercial investment. It will serve as the principal artery linking Laos and Thailand to China, and to other countries through China. There are already many vast hotel complexes and casinos on the country's borders, such as the special economic zone (SEZ) Ton Pheung in the Lao province of Bokeo.

The railway is projected to have forty-seven tunnels hewn through the mountains and numerous bridges, with a workforce of approximately 17,000 Chinese workers. Laos has a 30 percent stake in this venture, but lack of experience in building or managing railways means it cannot supply the manpower.

Trains will take ten hours to travel from Kumning to Vientiane, and will cut through northern and central Laos, passing through the most popular tourist destination, Luang Prabang. It cannot fail to affect both the economy and society, opening up the country to foreigners seeking investment opportunities in tourism and leisure. For the first time ever, all eyes are on Laos.

The second major project is the ongoing hydropower program to build many dams all along the Mekong River, the Nam Ou River, and others, in order to supply much-needed energy to Laos' large Southeast Asian neighbors. This will undoubtedly put Laos on the map. But at what risk? And to whose benefit, really? Mining is also having an impact in many areas of life in Laos.

This river is also the life pulse for the people of Laos, with many communities along its banks that rely on fishing and rice production for a living. Others toil in forestry and mineral extraction in the mountains, with many workers forced to accept migrant laboring or multiple jobs in order to survive. Some receive financial help from relatives abroad, and many still rely on basic services funded by foreign aid. Foreign aid is significant, and has one prime objective—to boost the economy.

LAOS TODAY

The newly emergent Laos is already in a fragile situation, with pressures from all sides: from tourism, and from powerful neighbors who are seeking to make use of Laos' vital resources and terrain with little regard for its inhabitants, their traditional means of livelihood, or the precious environment. There is the contrast of ongoing poverty—with children forced to work in the fields, lack of sanitation, health care, decent housing, and education—against the powerful corporations set on building huge hydropower stations and high-speed railways that cannot fail to bring Laos into the twenty-first century with a sometimes shocking and inevitably detrimental impact.

In addition, the population is facing a clash between traditional Lao religious principles and the official values of Lao Communist government. Quite a predicament!

In terms of migration, Lao people go to work in Thailand. Vietnamese workers migrate to Laos, although in relatively small numbers, primarily to work in the construction industry. Western foreigners come to work for embassies, NGOs, or the big engineering companies involved with hydropower, mining, and the like. Volunteers come and go, and others are setting up businesses connected to tourism and adventure activities.

chapter two

VALUES &
ATTITUDES

NATIONAL IDENTITY IN A GLOBALIZED WORLD

The people of Laos have long depended for their livelihood on agriculture and fishing, focusing on family, community, and keeping everyone housed and fed. They still use traditional methods of harvesting rice and catching fish, and the use of heavy machinery is quite rare. But things are starting to change.

The drive to create national identities in today's world can threaten the balance and tradition of ethnic groups who want to retain their individual identity and cultural heritage. Having an Issan–Lao "minority"—with, in essence, Lao language and culture—across the Mekong in Thailand, which outnumbers the entire population of Laos by three to one, illustrates the long-term and irreversible consequences of the way the map of this part of the world was drawn up by external forces. For many decades the Lao observed them from across the river—they could even hear the forbidden music floating over the water—envious of what seemed like a dream world in their neighboring country. Even today many wish they could work in cities like Bangkok. In contrast, there are others in the country who genuinely fear the collapse of traditional Lao values.

It is not easy for a country with possibly more than a hundred ethnic groups to become a nation with one common culture and language. However, the power of globalization is influencing even the social structure of the ethnic groups in Laos, and they are gradually merging under its impact. Many cannot fail to be affected by the presence of foreign visitors and business investors, or even those involved in voluntary work and foreign aid. And then there's another new force, or several—the presence of the Internet, new technology, and thriving industry just over most of the country's landlocked but also landlinked borders. What we are witnessing is the emerging of a nation that's been in a time warp. To give an example illustrating the forming of a nation-state in history, in as late as the year 1789 in France, only 50 percent of the population actually spoke French. They needed to nurture one official common language to interact together, which is what happened— and it is only now that this is happening in Laos.

This process has been, and will be, met with aversion, and sadly it will inevitably fracture some of the fragile ethnic, cultural, and linguistic heritage of Laos. The theoretical economic reform program implemented after the communists' unification of Laos in 1975 was intended to lead to more regional integration and greater awareness of its neighboring countries. It has become a question of adapting to modern times, so that foreigners today do not have to learn more than one language in order to interact with the people of Laos.

RELIGIOUS VALUES
Religion still pervades every aspect of life in Laos. Buddhism, animism, and ancestor worship are widely followed. The predominant religion, Theravada

Buddhism, was the state religion of the pre-republic Kingdom of Laos, during which time the *sangha*, the community of monks and novices, were on a par with the political hierarchy. More than half the population are Buddhists, mostly from lowland Lao. The Lao Theung and Lao Soung groups, which comprise two-fifths of the population, are primarily non-Buddhist. Animists venerate the spirits of, among others, mountains, lakes, day, night, and death. Although Buddhism and the local beliefs are not necessarily mutually exclusive, there have been many attempts to unify the religions. Local religious traditions are generally tolerated within the broader Buddhist community.

In the uplands, those who have migrated from southern China mix Confucian ideas with Buddhism and local religions. The Vietnamese, who occupy both the cities and the northeastern rural areas, practice a mixture of Mahayana Buddhism and Confucianism. And then there are other, smaller religious communities, which include Christians, Muslims, and followers of the Baha'i faith.

Although the country's constitution technically allows for freedom of religion, the post-revolution government has been known to restrict and interfere with this right, especially in the case of the minority religions, which have sometimes been labeled as "superstitious." In 1975 there was an attempt to take over the *sangha*, on the basis that they constituted a threat, and this resulted in many monks fleeing abroad. Since then the government has proceeded cautiously, even renovating temples and stupas in the country—in fact, as we have seen, the stupa was even substituted for the hammer and sickle in the national emblem!

Even today, other local religions may be more prevalent than official statistics cite, with many people professing to be Buddhists when in fact they consider Buddhism to be a culture rather than a religion. The most symbolic religious monuments are the temples, and they are everywhere—some magnificent and others a little dilapidated.

One of the most sacred Buddhist traditions that visitors enjoy viewing is the *Tak Bat*, an alms-giving ceremony carried out by the monks at dawn each day.

In the evenings the monks and novices chant together in Pali or Sanskrit, enunciating the words even though this is a foreign language that they don't understand at all. Ancient Buddhist scripture and doctrine were developed in several closely related literary languages of ancient India, particularly in Pali and Sanskrit.

Buddhist Monks

All Lao boys are expected to become monks for at least three months over their lifetime, and approximately a third of the male population used to be monks for life. They must have their heads shaved every full moon and they wear the traditional saffron-colored robes that have become so familiar to everyone.

It can be a harsh life for a young boy who is far from his home and family, but the benefits are an education and employment, which, particularly in the case of people from remote rural areas, would be impossible otherwise. The novices must obey seventy-five of the 227 rules of the monastic

order. They eat twice a day, at dawn and midday; much of the food is provided, and even pagodas are funded, by people seeking to accrue merit for a better *karma* in their next life. Important monks are also required to attend government seminars.

Boys and men are drawn to monkhood for various reasons other than the expected duty and a genuine commitment to their religion; sometimes someone who has just come out of hospital may join for a short period (three times a week, for example) to banish evil spirits; or there may have been a significant death in the family. Others are simply seeking better opportunities, and education is funded by the monasteries. Very few females join the monasteries.

CONFORMITY AND NONCONFRONTATION
Of all the experiences for visitors to Laos, the most significant is that they are witnessing the process of a nation entering the modern era. This involves great changes, and a shift away from the customs of a traditional, nonconfrontational society in which people

relied on advice and guidance from their elders and the religious hierarchy. Even the royal family would seek advice, not just in the early days but right up until the abolition of the monarchy in 1975.

When there was a conflict or serious difference of opinion, village leaders, village chiefs (*nai/nei ban* or *paw ban*) were called in to help. After 1975 that role was assumed by the nominated village presidents (*pathan ban*), who became heads of certain levels of administration and various committees linked to the totalitarian hierarchy. This practice still partially exists today, but the ancient title *nai/nei ban* has been restored. Old customs die hard, and many homes in Laos still contain shrines to Buddha and for offerings to various other spirits—always located above head level.

Conflict Resolution

Laotian people still speak softly and try to avoid confrontation. A loud voice is generally perceived as threatening. Their oral traditions convey lessons in moral integrity, life skills, and relationships—and what these days is called conflict resolution.

Highly respected non-family elders in the community were consulted for advice on how to resolve conflicts on their patch, either among families or neighbors. There was no such thing as going to law as people do in the modern world. The authority of these village elders was based on their honesty and on respect gained over long periods of time. They played a key role in conflict situations, where a confrontation would not achieve much, and conformity thus became a norm. These sage advisors often advised against confrontation, and herein lies the *boh pen nyang* philosophy of accepting and adapting to the situation. (See below, page 50).

NATIONAL SYMBOLS

Although only about 60 percent of the population in Laos are Buddhist, the principal national symbols are Buddhist. Before the revolution in 1975, the monarchy was also a key symbol. The regime then attempted to reduce these to solely secular national symbols, with a calendar that featured secular holidays only. Even then, they coincided with Buddhist celebrations. Following the death of communist leader Kaysone Phomvihane, the totalitarian government attempted to promote him to cult status, erecting statues to him all over the country. He is shown on six banknotes of the Lao currency, the kip.

Nowadays the country has reverted to its national symbols, with a renewed emphasis on the Buddhist religion. Since the revolution everyone celebrates National Day on December 2, but the That Luang Festival is once again the most important national event, celebrated over the full moon in November. The That Luang stupa in Vientiane is considered to be one of the most sacred places by all religious groups in Laos.

The royal Lao government first promoted these icons, including those of certain hill tribes in national costume and other Lao cultural features. This implied that other ethnic groups should slowly adapt to these symbols as well. There have been several debates about the gradual loss of the diversity of ethnic symbols from the past.

The Plain of Jars

There are other national Buddhist icons, but also some from other periods, such as the stone jars from the Plain of Jars from the megalithic era, dating back to the Iron Age and seemingly associated with prehistoric burial practices. The origin of these jars is still not entirely settled in archaeological terms. They are all located in Xiangkhouang Province, where more than ninety sites have been discovered, with as many as several hundred jars in some of them.

APPEARANCE MATTERS

These days, the people of Laos tend to wear Western clothing on an everyday basis. The national costume is worn only at festivals and for special events. The one exception is the women's skirt called a *sinh*, which is still often worn for work and on formal occasions, including by foreign residents. Sometimes you see people dressed up at local markets associated with special events too, but it may be that they wear their national dress because it is their finest clothing.

The ethnic tribes, particularly in the north of the country, have maintained the traditional hand weaving of silk and cotton garments, using natural dyes. Here, the wonderful intricate patterns and designs in a variety of bright colors continue to indicate the wearer's identity and social and marital status. In southern Laos, Savannakhet has distinctive Phou Thai cotton weaving, Champasak has high-quality silk weaving with patterns similar to some found in Cambodia, and Salavane, Sekong, and Attapeu specialize in banded cotton textiles with beads woven into the cloth.

Women and girls are very fashion- and makeup-conscious, particularly in the cities. Foreign visitors, who tend to dress more casually, are often surprised by the level of formal dress in banks and offices. This is yet another country where the locals try to keep their skin looking light and to protect it from the sun. Foreigners do the opposite and many take every opportunity to top up their tans, to the bemusement of the locals!

Many local motorcyclists can be seen wearing fascinating long-sleeved jackets with a tailor-made sewn extension to cover the upper section of their hands in the heat of the day, whose fabric is secured by a loop going under the thumb so that it does not restrict tricky maneuvering in the typically chaotic Asian traffic. Westerners have caught on, as you can be sitting on a motorbike for some time in heavy traffic with the sun scorching your skin, but they're inclined to use standard biking gloves ... so fashion trends are probably on the change!

Despite the fact that clothing is available at low prices, there are still many who can't afford to buy either garments or shoes. It is not unusual to spot a village child wearing odd shoes or two of quite different sizes.

BOH PEN NYANG

One of the first Lao expressions that visitors become familiar with is "*boh pen nyang*" (or "*bor pen yang*," or "*por pen yang*")—the spelling varies in accordance with the English or French legacy (unlike Vietnamese, the transliteration of Lao has never been formalized). Literally, it means "Not happening anything," or, word for word, "No is what"), but its multiple meanings can prove intriguing to foreigners, as it encompasses a range of possibilities, such as the affirmative "No problem" or "It doesn't matter; it's OK." Occasionally "*boh pen nyang*" conveys a confusing lack of commitment, as in "We can't do anything about it," but for the most part it is an upbeat expression used to end a phrase or situation, and a perfect reflection of the easygoing and fatalistic nature of the Lao people.

PERSONAL SPACE

People in Laos are sensitive about physical contact and personal space. They tend to keep at arm's length from each other, and any public display of affection (apart from the occasional holding of hands) is frowned on. Couples are cautious in public, and men and women make little direct eye contact with each other.

It is highly inappropriate to touch someone's head, unless this is an affectionate gesture toward a child. The head is considered the most sacred part of the body. If a person touches your head it means that they don't respect you. Even stretching over someone's head to reach something is considered very rude. People also have great respect for the elderly and for someone of authority, which is demonstrated by avoiding eye contact unless it is initiated by these people themselves. They also tend to stoop in a submissive fashion when passing someone senior to them.

STATUS, POWER, AND MONEY

What constitutes status in Laos has changed over the years. Once it was associated with kings, religious leaders, chieftains, or the heads of villages, whose positions were based on their heritage and leadership skills. These days, as all over the world, status seems to go hand-in-hand with the power of money. However, when it comes to Laos, traditional status still exists to a degree, meaning that it is not linked exclusively to money and the means of accumulating it, which for the average person was simply not possible.

In olden times in Laos, objects of personal wealth were items such as handcrafted wood and sandstone, pottery, pipes, a silk scarf or *sinh*, and jewelry. Now, and influenced by the country's rich neighbors and

SOME GESTURES AND TABOOS

- Don't point. It is considered rude.
- It is courteous and standard to remove your shoes before entering somebody's home, and compulsory when entering a Buddhist temple.
- Showing the soles of your bare feet is frowned on and deemed rude. Most Lao people are inclined to tuck their feet out of sight.
- It is taboo to touch a monk or his robe. Nothing can be handed to a monk directly, particularly if you are a woman. An example of this is perfectly illustrated in this true account: "Once we were parked within the *wat* grounds and looking for directions. A very courteous monk approached us and offered to help as he spoke a little English. We called our hosts at the guesthouse we were traveling to and invited the monk to talk to them on the phone. Much to our surprise he gestured that, before he could do this, any woman would have to place a cell phone on the ground before he could pick it up and help, thus avoiding direct contact."

Western tourists and corporate or NGO staff, a few Lao people have prospered and their wealth has taken on a different and more boastful side, with the appearance of grand houses, big, flashy cars and SUVs, and luxury clothing and goods bought on shopping trips abroad.

It is important to remember Laos' unique situation as a landlocked and isolated country for so many years. The monarchy was overthrown in 1975, and the country only started to open up again in the 1990s. Since then there has been limited economic growth, which has helped partially to reduce the level of poverty, but the country still relies on foreign aid.

When it comes to their work preferences, the people of Laos actively seek jobs in the civil service or with international companies, feeling that this will give them security. Needless to say, there are many who cannot even dream of this, and live in financially precarious circumstances.

According to the BBC country profile overview of Laos, less than 5 percent of the land is suitable for subsistence agriculture, and yet most of the population still lives in rural areas, struggling to survive where natural resources are diminishing through externally driven economic activity.

ATTITUDES TOWARD FOREIGNERS

It is difficult to generalize about the attitude of people in Laos toward foreigners, partly due to the presence of the many ethnic groups and their own traditional values that are so very different from those of the Western world. However, because they base their attitude on acceptance in most matters, this is reflected in their view of foreigners and their activities in Laos. Some of the older generation may feel resentment related to the largely undocumented impact of the Silent War; others may be bitter about the failures of certain internal poverty reduction projects, as described by the Australian academic Holly High in her book *Poverty and Policy in Laos*. Some resent their fellow countrymen who have been brought up abroad and returned prosperous and unscathed. Understandably, they also tend to view foreigners from different parts of the world in different ways because of the legacy of historic events and the particular roles of their countries in Laos over many years.

The Chinese

Historically, Chinese people have always been present in north Laos and the Mekong Valley, some being descendants of opium smugglers who settled in the province of Phongsali. Others were from a minority group known as the Ho from Yunnan Province in the People's Republic of China. Today the Chinese are now scattered all over Laos, working as laborers, merchants, and traders with a keen eye on the changing political situation and economic opportunities. And many more of their countrymen are moving across the border from their vast and densely populated homeland, whose population is 185 times that of Laos. They, too, are seeking business opportunities in an undeveloped country with growing potential alongside the industrial giant that is China.

Westerners

Western foreigners are nearly always extended a warm welcome and courtesy, and as a result of growing use of online media people in Laos are often in awe of those from what they consider to be sophisticated and wealthy countries. They have seen movies and know of famous celebrities. They assume that everyone is mega-rich, as visitors to their country often give that impression, traveling as they usually do on generous vacation budgets or earning substantial expat salaries—which in fact are far from representative of normal incomes in their home countries. The vast majority of people in Laos have never been out of the country, and can't

FARANG, FALANG, MANE FALANG

In many developing countries, especially those with a history of oral tradition, there is a "group name" for all foreigners. In Laos it is *farang* or *falang*, sometimes written with a capital letter and depicting foreigners as a "common nation," but also often written with a lowercase first letter, and used to describe "all white people grouped together." The term dates from French colonial times, when France as a country was called *Farang* in Lao. It is also used in Thai, indicating someone of European or American ancestry.

"Today Lao say *falang* when people are white and have big nose like European, American," was what an honest Lao friend replied when I asked what *falang* meant now. The etymology of the word can be traced even farther back in history, possibly from Hindi *firangi*, meaning foreign. It has also evolved differently, as in Khmer, where the term is *barang*. The government removed the letter "r" in 1975 from all the alphabets.

Another "specific characteristic" of foreigners is the different vegetables they eat, such as the potato, which people in Laos call *mane* (or *man*) *farang/falang*—"root vegetable of white people." The word *man(e)* is used to describe all kinds of starchy roots and tubers. Asparagus is called *noh-mai falang*, that is, "Western men bamboo shoots."

possibly aspire to do so for financial reasons, so they associate these countries with what they symbolize in terms of wealth and glamor. In the early '90s Lao people would call Westerners by their individual countries— "Latsia" (Russia), "Falanset" (*français*, or French), "Gelaman" (German). However, the Thai use only a single group determination, *farang*, and the Lao have started doing the same.

COPING AND ACCEPTANCE

The people of Laos tend to base their attitude on acceptance. A situation is what it is; you can't change it so why bother? They prefer to avoid discussion or confrontation. Part of this philosophy also stems from the Buddhist belief in reincarnation, meaning that they have to earn merit and accept their lot in this life, in anticipation of betterment in the "next life." There is also the traditional respect for hierarchy, which feeds into acceptance of the social situation. Westerners find some of these attitudes hard to understand and frustrating. A good example is in traffic, when a visitor has a near miss with an erratic local motorcyclist who doesn't indicate and simply reacts with a shrug and a placid smile. The easiest thing is to keep calm and carry on.

On an individual level they can be enterprising and hardworking, and undaunted in the face of setbacks.

RULES AND REGULATIONS

What rules and regulations? There are plenty of them, of course, but how much they are implemented is not very clear. There is still, for example, an official regulation regarding nightly curfews from 11:00 p.m.

onward, but it is rarely bothered with these days. The same goes for driving regulations such as wearing a motorcycle helmet or seat belt. What the eye doesn't see ...

GENDER RELATIONS

The Lao live in large, close-knit families, with several generations under the same roof, which tends to reinforce traditional social norms. Women used to dress modestly, and couples do not show affection in public. There is no cohabitation before marriage, and young people tend to marry in their mid to late twenties. Although they are free to choose their partners, the family usually has an important say in the matter. The official divorce rate is low.

In this conservative, traditional society, where extreme modesty is the norm for heterosexuals and homosexuality is not really visible, overtly sexual behaviour is not acceptable. But, human nature being what it is, people find a way and today are not always under such close scrutiny. What is done in private can no longer be controlled so easily by others.

chapter three

CUSTOMS &
TRADITIONS

The year in Laos revolves around festivals (*boun*), and, because the country has only recently opened up, visitors can still enjoy genuine cultural experiences. Thanks to the influence of the many diverse ethnic groups within this relatively small land, you will see great variety in festivals, customs, and costumes. This is no longer the case in many of the neighboring countries.

Festivals are based on the harvesting seasons, religious events, and the lunar calendar. They are frequently held during a full moon. Before the advent of modern transportation, villagers would walk for hours and even days to reach them, in eager anticipation of meeting people, exchanging news, and having a good time. They put all their worries aside for a few days, and this is still the case today. Although religion plays an important role, the fact is that Laos loves a party!

Then there are the smaller celebrations: weddings, baptisms, homecomings, farewells, and funerals are all reasons to arrange a gathering. Many temples and sacred stupas also have their own special festivals.

The passing down of Lao and ethnic tribal traditions, customs, and history through the

generations has been by word of mouth, as opposed
to any written form. Hopefully this will continue,
particularly as economic and educational progress
means that more and more customs are now being
recorded for posterity in hard or digital format.

CUSTOMS

Although Buddhism is the predominant religion in
Laos, it is often combined with other customs, rituals,
and religions that go back many generations and
centuries, particularly in remote areas where people
are isolated from modern trends that affect the urban
areas. This fascinating religious syncretism is not
always apparent to foreigners from the developed
world. It's not just a matter of not understanding the
language—it's the difficulty of grasping the essence of
their culture and traditional customs.

So, alongside Buddhism and the stupas or temples
that mark each village and town, homage may also
be paid to protective spirits. Altars are built for them,
and there are accompanying rituals with chants,
drums, horns, and music, and even animal sacrifices
made to ward off evil spirits. Few foreigners get to
witness these scenes.

In larger urban areas the stupas may be quite
grand and painted in gold, while village temples
vary and are often built from simple materials.
Nevertheless, they are still the focal point for
offerings and feasts, organized in keeping with the
Buddhist belief in the performance of good works,
right living, and supporting temples and shrines to
hasten the attainment of *nirvana* at the final level
of reincarnation.

Traditional Clothing

The handwoven *sinh* is a traditional garment worn by women. It's basically a tube-shaped skirt, made from silk, cotton, or nowadays even synthetic fabric. Women wear it in various ways, and the design and color can vary, denoting a special event within their ethnic group, social status, and where they are from. The

skirt itself is generally two-tone, while the hem has all the intricate design detail. Many foreign women living in Laos used to wear only *sinh* skirts to work, particularly for formal occasions.

On Laos National Day, December 2, an annual rally is held at sports stadiums. It starts at first light and different ethnic groups proudly parade in wonderful traditional costumes with large banners glorifying the nation.

BACI, OR *SOU KHUAN*

Baci (*basi*, *baasi*), or *Sou Khuan* (*Su Kwan*, *Sukhuan*), meaning "calling of the soul," is a ritual for summoning wandering spirits. It is often described as an ethnic Lao ritual, a traditional ceremony representing the very centerpiece of Lao culture, but it also exists in Isan Thai culture. People in Laos perform it as a welcome to a visitor, for marriage, a birth, returning home, any of the annual festivals, as well as modern and professional events such as the opening of a new office or the arrival of new staff. Those who are ill are given *bacis* to help heal them, officials are honored by *bacis*, and novice monks are bestowed luck with a *baci* before entering the temple.

The ceremony is held on any day of the week, and generally before either midday or sunset. It is based on the Buddhist belief that our bodies comprise thirty-two organs (which can be grouped in different ways); the *baci* ritual of "calling of the soul," or *kwan*, acts as the vital force to protect and restore balance and harmony between them.

The central part of the ritual entails tying white cotton strings around people's wrists. Anyone can tie these strings on someone close to them, wishing them luck with an encouraging smile. Sometimes a banknote is tied to the string to be given to the host.

Baci is also widely practiced by foreigners, with Westerners living in Laos organizing *baci* ceremonies on moving into their house, or as a leaving party

for their house staff or friends. Often Westerners can be seen with a dozen or more strings attached to their wrists, which they wear with pride as evidence of having taken part in this lovely symbolic event. International schools and expat communities celebrate *baci* for good luck at the start of the school year or as a farewell at the end. It is an ideal opportunity for staff and families to meet.

Pah kwan forms part of the ceremony. This is an eye-catching symbolic arrangement of leaves and flowers with white cotton and some silk threads laid out on a large dish, bowl, or tray, often prepared by the elderly women members of the family. It also contains food for the *kwan* set out around the base, which is made of banana leaves adorned with orange flowers. At the end of the ceremony the festive food is offered to all the guests, and can be accompanied by the traditional music and dance.

TAK BAT, ALMS-GIVING CEREMONY

During the morning Buddhist monks in their saffron robes process along the streets with their begging bowls, and people come out to give them food. This ancient tradition is one of the most photogenic sights. Today, however, it is sometimes overcrowded and in danger of losing its solemnity.

As one scholar has remarked, "Exposure to tourism and social contact with tourists is influencing the values and aspirations of the city's many monks, as evidenced by trends such as monks eschewing the study of traditional skills in favor of foreign languages to help them enter the tourism industry."

The donation of "money trees" can form part of different rituals. Festooned with long chains of banknotes, sometimes individually wrapped in cellophane, which can be bought prepared for the occasion, these are presented to the temples, which are considered to be spiritual channels to the deceased. Village elders often perform the chanting.

NEW YEAR

Laos welcomes two new years each year—the Gregorian in January and the Buddhist in April. The traditional lunar Buddhist calendar, which is 543 years ahead of the Gregorian calendar, is still used in Laos. This intriguing dual calendar system is evident

in the LED-light signs in the urban areas. Calendars
with elements of both systems are still printed for
the international banks, and both Laos and Thailand
continue to use the Buddhist calendar in daily life.

Buddhist New Year (Boun Pi, Pii Mai Lao, or Songkran)

The phases of the moon are of special significance
in Buddhism, and specific full moon days are times

of celebration. The New
Year starts on the first full
moon in April. This is the
most important event in
Laos, and celebrations are
held all over the country.
Officially it usually falls on
April 15, 16, and 17, but
the festivities can go on for
as long as a week. This is
also the start of spring and
the welcome rain for crops.
It is a wonderful experience
for visitors, who are swept
up in the lively and colorful
throng as many people
converge to meet up with family and friends.

The first day is taken up with preparation.
Perfumed water is collected, and the Buddha images
are placed in more accessible areas in the *wats*, where
offerings are left and the images are carefully washed
by worshipers, who then take the rest of the water
home to use in blessing and purifying their own
family and friends, wishing them well for the coming
year. The protective spirits are also invoked, and the
traditional horn and mouth organ are played.

Next day, every house is cleaned to ward off any evil spirits, and young people are encouraged to go out and bathe their elders before getting wet themselves, in order to banish all the negative elements of the past year. It is also a time when caged animals and birds are released from captivity.

On the third day many *bacis* will be held to usher in the New Year with blessings, good wishes, and gifts bestowed on the elders, who are asked for forgiveness if their families feel that they have hurt or offended them in any way. In the evening the Buddha images are returned to their usual places in the *wats*, and there, through the monks' acts of chanting and also pouring water over them, they are asked for forgiveness for having been handled over the past few days.

Water is symbolic as a vital cleanser, and everyone gets extremely wet during the Lao New Year celebrations—not just by being doused with water, but also by being thrown into makeshift pools and the river. In the old days, only women were allowed to throw men into the water, but now it's a free for all, with a great

deal of smiling and laughter. As it's so hot nobody
generally minds, but make sure your valuables are in
waterproof bags, and go with the flow!

In the larger towns and cities there is a real carnival
feel, with music, parades, pagodas, face painting,
masks, and even beauty pageants. Markets and food
stalls are all buzzing. There is a great deal of drinking,
and the traffic and driving are crazier than ever.

In Vientiane there are vast sandbanks on the
Mekong River that are accessible, thanks to the low
water level at this time of year. Here people build high
sand castles, decorate them with good-luck symbols,
and bathe to wash away their worries and ask for
blessings and luck in the coming year.

Chinese New Year

This is also celebrated in Laos, following the lunar
calendar and falling between late January and
early February. It is believed that the spirits of one's
ancestors return for the day. There are always many
flowers and fireworks.

International New Year

The international New Year is recognized too, but really only for official purposes and in deference to Westerners. Many foreign residents and families are away at this time of the year.

Hmong New Year

At the beginning of December, this proud ethnic group displays its unique heritage in colorful and ornate traditional clothing made from green, red, and white silk, decorated hats, and handmade silver jewelry. There is music and dancing, with traditional instruments such as the *teun*-flute, Hmong-style *khene* pipe, and leaf blower. There are games such as *makkhon* (cotton-ball throwing), and spinning-top races, crossbow demonstrations, and ox fighting.

LAO NATIONAL DAY

Lao National day is held on December 2 to mark the abolition of the monarchy and the creation of the Lao People's Democratic Republic in 1975. This mandatory public holiday is marked with military parades and speeches to acknowledge the country's history and celebrate its independence.

BUDDHIST LENT

The Buddhist Lent retreat coincides with the annual three-month rainy season, during which monks stay in their monasteries to study and meditate, and one should practice self-discipline and abstention. Some people give up drinking alcohol during this period. It is also very uncommon to hold marriage celebrations during Buddhist Lent.

BOUN THAT LUANG

The Great Stupa, That Luang, in Vientiane is the national symbol of Laos and the country's most sacred monument, built in 1566. Old postcards show it surrounded by lush tropical vegetation and trees, but now it is completely walled in, with a magnificent soaring spire covered in gold leaf.

It is here that one of the most important festivities is held in November over a period of three days during full moon. Thousands of people in Laos (and Thais, Vietnamese, and Cambodians) travel from all over to visit the shrines, which contain relics of Buddha, and visitors can witness a stunning assembly of pilgrims dressed in their best clothes gathering solemnly together before dawn. They listen to hundreds of priests from many different *wats* chanting and praying in this revered place of worship.

The festivities include a fantastic firework display. This is a must-see, but be warned, there are a lot of people everywhere and it can be overwhelming. Throughout there are also impressive processions with wax castles, which are carried around the stupas and offered at the shrines.

There is a great conflict of sound, with many loudspeakers blaring out different announcements at the same time and absolutely no control. Within the temple, contributors' names are called out, detailing the names and amounts in what sounds a bit like a lottery call—with interesting pronunciations of the foreign names!

As this is a multinational event, there are many ASEAN stands promoting their own countries, as well as markets offering all sorts of merchandise and food.

BOUN BANG FAY

Boun Bang Fay, also spelled "Fai," is a rocket festival held in May, before the rainy season, in the Vientiane area and surrounding villages in the south. Wonderful homemade rockets are set off as a way of asking the gods for plenty of rain and good harvests. Decorated bamboo sticks are rammed with gunpowder, and the more adventurous youngsters clamber up the fragile structures to light them, getting dangerously close before the sticks shoot up into the air and explode. This festival evolved from pre-Buddhist fertility rites to encourage the coming of the rains, and is full of bawdy humor. There is plenty of music and dancing, with processions of decorated floats over about three days of celebrations. In some villages the men blacken their faces with soot, while women wear sunglasses and wooden phallus carvings to imitate the menfolk.

ELEPHANT FESTIVAL

Laos was called "the Land of a Million Elephants" (Lan Xang) for a reason, and these magnificent beasts have

long been a national symbol, loved and respected by all and previously an integral part of the working community. However, as a result of modernization and the reduced need for them in traditional work in the forests, plus the devastating deforestation of their natural habitat in recent years, the elephant population has dwindled. In the year 2006 an NGO that had worked with elephants for many years had the idea of organizing an elephant festival to promote awareness of them and their plight in the face of modernization.

The festival is now held every February in Xayabouri (Sayabouri), a region well known for its strong tradition of training and handling elephants. Since then the local government has also become involved in the organization of this fantastic gathering of up to a hundred elephants, attracting more than 80,000 visitors to this normally quiet little village for several days.

The elephants are adorned with beautiful mats and intricate embroidered headdresses, some extending from the tops of their heads right down their trunks. Sometimes their faces or hides are painted with stunning designs. It is a wonderful experience to watch them majestically ambling along with shaded wicker seats or bright parasols protecting their passengers from the sun. Proud *mahouts* sit behind their ears, dressed in traditional costume. The elephants are fed bananas and sugar cane, laid out on tables in front of them.

There are colorful processions with elephant dressage, music, and dancing, all dominated by these gracious walking giants. Note the hierarchy that is observed, and don't miss watching the elephants bathe in the river at sunset and sunrise.

OTHER OFFICIAL HOLIDAYS AND IMPORTANT EVENTS

International Women's Day (March 8)

This is a day that pays tribute to all Laotian women, when supposedly they rest and their menfolk assume their duties. It is respected by all administrations and, if it falls on a weekend, an extra day off is granted on the Monday. Some suggest that you avoid visiting administrative offices the next day, as revelers may still be feeling fragile!

Labor Day (May 1)

Labor Day is a public holiday in many countries worldwide to celebrate the achievements of workers, often linked with trade union movements, and it is an important government celebration in Laos. On this day communist flags are more evident than usual.

Boun Souang Heua (Lao Long Boat Racing)

This event takes place at the end of the rainy season and the Buddhist Lent (in fall, around October/November) on the Mekong River in places like Vientiane, Luang Prabang, or Savannakhet. This a fun time for everyone, with teams from different villages and districts traveling from all over to compete in long boats carved from one

tree, painted in bright colors with intricate designs, many with carved dragon figureheads at the prow. They are considered sacred vessels and, like the other festivals in Laos, the boat race is held to honor the water divinities and *nagas* (see page 74). There can be up to fifty paddlers to a boat, with the women competing in the morning and the men in the afternoon. They race in heats and the prizes are both money and trophies. Enjoy the buzz with traditional drums, chanting, dancing, and concerts. There are markets, food—and a lot of loud music!

LAI HEUA FAI (LIGHT FESTIVAL)

This wonderful festival also happens at the end of Lent everywhere in Laos. *Lai heua fai* means "floating boats of light downstream," so it helps if there is a river nearby! Everyone asks their *nagas* for good luck in the coming year, and the villagers decorate floats with fantastic swirling dragon shapes made from paper, and decked with flowers, incense, and candles, which parade in a candlelit procession through the town and down to the river bank.

Dragon Boat Racing on the Mekong

One of my most enriching experiences in Laos was taking part in a dragon boat race. I started with what were supposed to be weekly training sessions for about two months, although this wasn't always easy to organize. I was in a very informal international women's team, and the training took place in the village of Ban Sai Fong Neua, a thirty-minute drive from Vientiane, very much off the beaten path. Thanks to team members with 4x4 cars, we safely navigated the narrow, bumpy tracks through the forest, and picked our way through washing lines and makeshift dwellings down to the river, where wide-eyed children swam and gaped at the foreigners.

One thing you will certainly learn when rowing in a dragon boat is how to count in Lao, as, with up to fifty of us in the boat, we all had to count as loudly as possible in order to coordinate the rowing. This was also a time when we learned a lot more about the need for flexibility, and a certain relaxed attitude toward rules, which were certainly bent a bit!

Despite its technically being an international women's team, as there weren't enough of us in the team the village girls (and boys!) joined in. Nobody dared to ask if this mixed crew would be allowed to participate, though we fervently hoped so. Somehow it happened regardless, and a combination of foreign and local rowers of all ages raced.

The somewhat informal attitude to rules and regulations came as a bit of a surprise, but there was no hint of foul play. We were all delighted to race together and had a lot of fun, despite the language barrier and getting extremely muddy and wet!

Nagas are Buddhist deities that take the form of great snakes. In Laotian mythology they are female snakes with magical powers that live in the rivers. They are revered by all as life-givers, and water is a particularly vital source of life.

There are brightly lit lanterns and candles wherever you look—on the floats, on the ground, swinging from posts, and held by people in the parades. The floats are ceremonially set alight, then launched on to the water and cast adrift. Flower offerings on small platforms are also launched on to the water, and the whole atmosphere is electric.

FAMILY OCCASIONS

Most important family occasions are marked with a big celebration that can last several days, and tend to cost a lot, meaning that families either draw from their savings or borrow the money.

A Traditional Lao Marriage

Marriage traditions vary in accordance with the culture of the many ethnic groups throughout Laos. It is always a joyous event, attended by many relatives and generally held at the bride's house. The morning has always been deemed a happier time for weddings in Laos, but these days people have to adapt to their work schedule and many weddings are held in the afternoon.

Traditionally, after the proposal, known as *sou khor,* an envoy was sent to the bride's family to request her hand in marriage officially and offer a bride price of money or gold. There was also an *oung dong,* which is a type of "marriage warming" party, which only close friends and relatives attend. They help with the wedding preparations, preparing the customary decorative *pah*

kwan flower arrangement and food. The mother of the bride or an older respected female member of the family will prepare the marital bed. Both bride's and groom's family homes are blessed, and normally the couple lives with her family for the first year. For the ceremony they wear beautiful traditional wedding clothes, with the bride in white Lao silk with gold adornments, and the groom wearing a white or cream silk shirt.

The *baci* blessing at the beginning of the ceremony is moving, with chanting, the couple feeding each other an egg, and tying white strings on each other's wrists to unite them. The festivities generally last two days.

Birth

Birth and death are important events, and traditions vary according to ethnic group. For the first three or four weeks after birth talismans and other objects may be used, and this period is called *you deuane*. Most mothers still comply with certain traditions, such as not eating meat and having a kind of herbal burner under the bed for many days in order to dry out the womb. The *you kham* ceremony is about the mother recovering from birth and regaining her internal strength.

Death

Death is readily accepted in Laos, as Buddhists believe that one simply moves on to one's next life. The body is usually placed in a coffin, generally laid out at home, and visitors come to pay their respects, dressed in somber clothing and bearing gifts of simple food and even money. After the cremation there is a series of traditional ceremonies. After weddings, funerals are the most costly events for families.

The body is always cremated, and great deference is shown at this event, with many people attending from afar to take part in the prayers and the ceremony. The valuables of the deceased are often placed alongside them, but once the cinders have cooled the ashes are placed in an urn and anything that survives the fire, such as gold, is retrieved. Three days later, in accordance with Buddhist practice, merit-making deeds and alms offerings to monks often take place.

People in Laos are genuinely surprised by Westerners' approach to illness and death. They remain particularly caring of their elderly, believing it to be their duty to look after them at home until they die, and also to ensure that the body is there until it is cremated.

They often question why we leave our deceased to be prepared for burial by hospital or undertaking staff and mourn them in a different way.

SPIRITS

Social life and the rhythm of family life in Laos are heavily influenced by religious practices. Belief in spirits and ancestor worship are at the heart of their religions and predate the arrival of Theravada Buddhism, which absorbed many earlier practices. Spirits are known to inhabit "common places" in nature—earth, water, stones, rice paddies, forest, mountains—and areas that are important in daily life, protecting villages or homes.

At times, specific objects and even musical instruments can house spirits. The Hmong, for example, systematically play instruments that they believe to contain house spirits. There is a specific piece of music to be played on the *khene* (mouth organ) each time it is used, that is dedicated to the instrument's spirit,

Many people still believe in a variety of spirits, both good and evil, that either command respect and honor or need to be tamed or driven away.

Clinics and hospitals have had an impact on the ancient and traditional reliance on asking spirits for help with ill health, and many Lao people now gratefully place their faith in doctors and nurses. Nevertheless, locals still hold rituals too, praying to spirits, begging for forgiveness, and making offerings and sacrifices to cure ailing relatives, particularly within ethnic groups, such as the Tai Dam, in remote areas. Where Westerners question illness and want scientific answers, these gentle people tend to blame it on *karma*, or the possibility that they are being punished by the family's protective spirit for some offense.

chapter four

MEETING PEOPLE

The people of Laos focus on their family and the traditional tightly knit community, where, for decades and despite modern progress in most other places in the world, they were largely isolated by the lack of transportation. Nowadays, a laborer might have a motorbike to get him to work and to take his wife to a market that is farther away, but mostly people stay where they are and there is little opportunity for friendship outside the community.

MAKING FRIENDS

Foreign visitors and expatriate workers will find themselves associating with people from their own and other countries who speak their own language and understand their way of life. There are social gatherings in cafés, guesthouses, hotels, international schools, libraries, social and professional expat get-togethers, and fundraising events. Local people that foreigners meet in in these settings are largely from the minority who can afford this type of luxury or who have been invited to some of these events.

We are here, of course, talking about urban areas such as Vientiane and Luang Prabang, where locals are used to the presence of foreigners. Living in or even just visiting the mountains or countryside is a very different experience, and in the remote areas foreigners are rarely seen. This means that meeting and interacting with their inhabitants can be an exceptional experience. You may be invited to join in a local event in a rural area; if you are there is no way of knowing whether it will be in an open space, communal venue, or someone's home.

Online dating is growing fast in Laos both between local people and with foreigners, thanks to modern communications. People establish their preferences and get to know each other online before meeting face to face. The Lao no longer rely on advice traditionally asked from elders and religious and community leaders.

INTERACTING WITH THE PEOPLE

Laotian people are naturally curious, although owing to the country's political history they were subdued and reticent for years. That's all changing now, and they enjoy talking to foreigners. However, the language barrier can be a major obstacle, also highlighting the disparity between those who have had a dismal education and others from a privileged background who have learned a foreign language.

Meeting people casually is one thing; it's another to get to know them. While the people of Laos are warm and welcoming, it is rare to be invited into their homes, as generally they hold family events outdoors. You may be offered a drink on the porch, but they will be wary of revealing their modest living quarters. They will be courteous and curious, but it is important to accept that generally we come from very different places and backgrounds, that they may view us with some awe and have little true understanding of who we are, and that many of them cannot afford the kinds of leisure activities that Westerners take for granted when socializing.

However, if you do make friends with a Lao family, they may well drop in on you unannounced, probably completely oblivious of your hospitality protocol and visiting you just because they happen to be close by. And when you do invite them, there's no knowing if they'll arrive on time.

French was the principal academic and government language until 1975, and this legacy is still evident now, with many older government officials still in position who are completely fluent in French, and some of whom were even educated in France. In the period after 1975, Russian and other Eastern European languages became more evident as people in Laos were offered the chance to study in those countries. It is not uncommon to meet people of that generation who have lived in Czechoslovakia or maybe Poland, but although they might mention it and say that they speak Eastern European languages, they generally appear reluctant to discuss what was clearly a difficult experience.

Traditional Values

People in Laos still maintain their traditional moral values and integrity, and that religion plays a large role, with great respect being paid to monks. For Westerners this is a real eye opener, as it highlights the changes in our own globalized world.

The natural acceptance of life in the face of poverty and hardship is genuinely humbling. The people of Laos try to forget their recent political history and dream of a better life, waiting quietly and patiently for it to come about.

Joining in Sports and Games

One of the most natural and enriching ways to interact with the local population is through sports. These can range from football to handball, or even races, and games where anyone around simply joins in—foreign children who live in or close to a local neighborhood, a voluntary medical doctor, or young NGO volunteers joining a football game. Everyone can enjoy sports and manage without knowing the language—it's enough to get involved and have fun, and it makes for great memories.

GREETINGS

Sabaidee! is the most common greeting and probably one of the most important phrases to remember in the standard Lao language. Literally meaning "It goes well," it is used for both social and business encounters.

People in Laos show great courtesy and respect, using the deferential *nop* greeting—hands clasped in a prayerful gesture followed by a slight bow, and avoiding eye contact with superiors—but they are very curious about foreigners, and often ask disconcerting questions straight away, such as how old you are and if you are married. In social interactions, the *nop* was discouraged after the revolution, but is omnipresent once again.

HOSPITALITY

People in Laos take pride in their family events, and foreign guests are often welcome to attend. Sometimes an invitation to a formal family occasion will be given just a few days in advance—although your host will also give you a printed invitation to follow Western protocol and to keep as a memento. They will, however, expect everyone to know about it automatically through the traditional family and village communication network, via word of mouth.

Everyone dresses up for the occasion and, in the case of the wealthier locals, parties can be very lavish. At the beginning of their stay in Laos, foreign guests tend to wear only Western dress, but as time goes on, both men and women *falang* enjoy buying and wearing beautiful custom-made Laos clothing such as the *sinh* skirt and handwoven silk ceremonial sashes, tops, and shirts.

In Laos, businesses and associations often host extravagant parties or events, which come within their general budget. Foreign guests may find this disconcerting in view of the country's social and economic situation, but it would be offensive not to attend.

Where Are You Going? Just Walking Around . . .
In Laos a typical greeting is "Where are you going?" rather than "How are you doing?" To which the standard reply is "*Khoy (koi) pay (pai) lin*," meaning "I'm going for a walk (or to play)."

Foreigners tend to be taken aback by such a direct question as a conversation opener, instead of a simple "Hello," but soon learn that this is just a relaxed form of greeting that you can respond to with courtesy and get on with whatever you were doing.

VISITING A LAO HOME
The people of Laos are very hospitable and enjoy offering food and drinks. Even short-term visitors are often invited to join in major family celebrations.

However, while one might be invited to events held in temples or different venues, it is not usual to be invited to a private home. With growing prosperity for some Lao, however, those with new homes, staff, and Western-style furniture like it all to be seen. Note that local people may be reluctant to invite foreigners to stay at their house overnight because this is still frowned upon by the police and governing bodies.

Shoes Off!

On entering a home in Laos, guests remove their shoes and leave them outside the house or on the stairs. It's the same in small stores and in restaurants that form part of somebody's home. If you see a pile of shoes outside a shop, guesthouse, or home that you want to enter, leave yours there too. This custom might not always be obvious, and there is rarely a sign outside asking people to remove their footwear. As a general rule of etiquette anywhere in Asia, if you see a shoe rack, or shoes lined up outside, your best bet is to remove yours as well. Some shops offer rattan slippers for you to wear inside.

Dining Etiquette

When visiting Laotian homes, or even offices, guests are usually offered water, and it is polite to accept, even if you're not thirsty. Take a sip to be polite, even if you don't drink the whole glass. When dining, Lao people will often assume you have finished eating if you begin to drink water from your glass.

Respect and honor, we have seen, are shown to elders in the community, and deference is demonstrated by height, meaning that any person of a lesser age or position should always be beneath their immediate eye level. In the past, if the elders were sitting on the floor, then visitors were expected to do the same, and often guided to a mat to sit on. Nowadays they're more likely to be sitting on chairs, with younger members of the family on mats on the floor. When sitting on the floor, men tend to sit cross-legged; the women fold their legs to one side. Tea or water or fruit will probably

be offered, and it would be rude not to accept. Household staff mostly avoid eye contact, and often gently crouch when passing by someone who is seated.

For meals, everyone sits on mats on the floor, and they may squat down to serve you, honoring the tradition of keeping their heads below the level of their guests'. Avoid stepping over anyone, or their food, as this is frowned on and they might not eat it.

People in Laos always wash their hands thoroughly before eating. They eat using their fingers, but also use a fork and spoon: the fork in the left hand and the spoon in the right. For sticky rice they use only their right hand and fingers, shaping the rice into a ball and dipping it into dishes to mop up morsels and juice. They use chopsticks and a spoon for noodles and noodle soup.

GIFT GIVING

What to take along? It depends on the event, but for more informal parties (to which Lao people almost always bring food) a token gift that originates from your country is always welcome—such as a typical ornament or souvenir, wine, or perfume. Fruit is also appreciated as an informal gift, as it can be a luxury item for some families. Gifts should always be offered with the right hand.

In the case of name-givings or weddings, cash gifts are widely accepted. Money is placed in an envelope (the one containing the invitation card is often used for this), and left in a special box at the party venue. The amount of money given depends on the connection with the bride and groom and their families.

Thank-you notes are sure to be appreciated, but are not strictly necessary. The people of Laos tend to express their thanks with reciprocal favors and gifts.

Foreigners are sometimes taken aback to be offered gifts of potentially threatened flora and fauna, such as carved ivory or leather goods made from endangered species. These may not be allowed out of the country.

INTERNATIONAL MEETING POINTS

Because Laos, and particularly its urban areas, has a relatively small population, visitors from different countries end up meeting a lot of people from different walks of life. Interacting with locals is the best way of gaining an insight into Laotian society and, as we've seen, people in Laos are open, curious, and welcoming. But foreigners like meeting other foreigners too, and in a funny way have a different common language, based not on what language they speak but on how they think, because of their education and background in modern democratic countries.

When it comes to meeting up with other foreigners and local expats, it's a small world here, and everyone socializes in the same places. Apart from hotels and backpacker venues (where people keep on meeting as they follow the same travel loop around the country), restaurants, and cafés, there are exhibition openings, cultural evenings, debates, and other events, often posted online or in the social media. At these places you might be chatting with anybody—high-ranking officials, diplomats, academics, doctors, business entrepreneurs, and volunteers.

There are embassy events too, such as the German embassy's cinema and cultural gatherings. This building is centrally located and makes a perfect venue, with the added interest of having being the East German embassy during the Cold War. The Russians get together in another well-located embassy in a huge building from the 1980s.

The French organize many cultural events, often accompanied by irresistible *cuisine française*. They maintain their long-standing legacy of colonial

influence and various cultural institutions dating way back, such as the French School of Asian Studies, École Française d'Extrême-Orient (EFEO), founded in 1900 in Saigon. There has long been a traditional French/English language divide, but as time goes on, and with the strong Australian and ASEAN influence in Laos, it is the English language that now seems to dominate. Just another example of *boh pen nyang*!

PRIVATE & FAMILY LIFE

THE FAMILY

Life in Laos is inevitably changing as the country opens up, but even now only Vientiane and the other provincial capitals are what Westerners would consider to be urban, and they function mainly as administrative centers rather than industrial ones.

The family unit remains a very important factor, where people are bound by love and still retain a great sense of duty and honor toward the older generation and those relatives who are worse off, both economically and health-wise. It is a pleasure to witness these strong links in urban and rural areas alike, particularly in the face of ongoing poverty and even a lack of food in some areas.

The women focus on the home and keeping everyone fed, while the men work in the fields, although women frequently help out on the land at harvest time or on the river whenever necessary. Work, school vacations, religious festivals—all revolve around rice, the primary crop and staple food, which is produced from the start of the rainy season in April or May until the end of the monsoon season in September or October. The monsoon period is also a hugely influential factor in all sectors of the country.

Children assist with menial daily tasks when they are not at school, and with small-trade produce or handicrafts. The boys will soon start helping their

fathers, and the art of weaving cotton and silk has been passed down from women to their daughters since the fourteenth century.

Everyday existence can be very harsh. The menfolk are known to overindulge at times with beer or *lao lao*, an alcoholic drink distilled from rice. And unlike in some neighboring countries, there is little social stigma against women and children joining in the drinking culture. Children's growth may be stunted from malnutrition and bearing loads such as water and heavy produce from a young age. It is worth remembering that the people of Laos are accepting of their lot, thanks to the predominant Buddhist faith, and that the expression *"boh pen nyang"* illustrates this philosophical outlook extremely well.

THE RHYTHM OF RURAL LIFE
The daily lives of rural people involve a number of tasks, many linked to agricultural activities that are strictly

seasonal. They also hunt for game, fetch water from rivers and wells, and gather various forest products. Many forest products remain essential for daily subsistence: birds and eggs, fruit and honey, small game, herbs, spices and medicines, and wood for fuel, for making charcoal, resins, latex, and dyes. Women are often associated with the gathering and processing of forest products. The forest is also a source of structural materials such as wood, rattan, bamboo, and different fibers.

Lao villages are close to their principal means of livelihood, such as rice paddies, upland fields, fishing, or forestry, with new families joining if they have been driven from their former homes by relocation or other external factors. The houses are set close together, generally built on stilts in a combination of wood and cement blocks with thatched or corrugated pitched roofs. The villages vary in size from a cluster of small houses or dwellings, occupied by people who are all related, to numerous households of many families originating from different parts of the region. *Muang* towns (*muang/mueang*, town, in both Thai and Lao) have emerged as trading, market, and administrative centers. They may have up to 5,000 inhabitants, often including a mix of ethnic groups, dominated by Lao.

In the last century Buddhism was omnipresent and of extreme importance in everyday village life, and Buddhist monks played a vital role as advisers and healers. The villagers' central point of worship is the *wat/vat*, the temple, or sacred precinct, and they still rely heavily on the monks for advice on all aspects of local social, economic, and health issues. The monks are often natural healers but, interestingly, many of them were warriors at some point in their lives.

Nai ban, the village chief, plays an important guiding and advisory role, and in addition he receives and administers the local taxes. Religious festivals draw them and other neighboring villages together. Family gatherings may also bring guests from elsewhere, when the work of preparing the food is shared by the guests, family, and close neighbors.

Children of different age groups can be seen playing close to school areas, by the *wat* grounds, or on the porches of the larger houses. As it is only in recent years that Laos has opened up to tourists, people living in the rural villages are particularly fascinated by foreigners, gathering around them out of sheer curiosity, and certainly not to beg for money or gifts.

About 90 percent of rural villagers cultivate rice, with many also growing vegetables and fruit and keeping chickens and livestock, plus perhaps a pair of buffalo or cattle to plow or pull a cart. Some grow tobacco and mulberries. Although there are growing market prospects, subsistence farming is still the most common type throughout the small villages in the country. Work and access to food varies in accordance with seasonal crops, weather, and the harvesting periods, so many villagers will also hunt for small game and birds or gather wild foods such as bamboo, mushrooms, roots, and leaves, which can be medicinal too. They make their own tools and clothing, they weave cloth and baskets, and trade or sell any surplus to stock up on less easily obtainable items such as medical supplies,

soap, fuel, and household goods. Only about a third of villages have their own food markets.

There is no doubt that modern technology and globalization have made their mark on many villages in Laos. It is impossible for young people in particular not to be influenced by the power of the Internet and social media. However, the village structure is still intact outside the urban areas, based on the age-old tradition of sharing the good and the bad as a community, with everyone looking out for not just their immediate family but neighbors as well. There is the utmost respect for hierarchy, still evident in some villages through the design of the woven fabric of their clothing, which also indicates family and social ranking.

Village inhabitants do come and go. Some of the boys may be chosen as monks and go to monasteries, which is a great source of pride for the whole village. Others leave for economic reasons, or because they have relatives who persuade them to move to their area. In addition, entire villages have been broken up by resettlement.

Weaving in the Household

An important village activity in Laos is the making of traditional textiles and clothing. These fabrics are intricately dyed and woven by hand, from wild silk or cotton. Many rural homes have looms, built by the menfolk under their houses, and it is here that the women set to work and weave, using beautiful natural colors and bold traditional geometric designs.

HOUSES AND APARTMENTS

The house and home are sacred to people in Laos. In addition to the people living in a house, it is also inhabited by the house spirit, which serves as its guardian but also punishes those who defy certain house rules.

Lao architecture is a mixture of traditional wooden houses set on stilts with sloping roofs; elegant French

colonial style houses with tiled roofs and louvred shutters on the windows and doors; and, increasingly, modern urban-style housing and apartments. This is where the traditional wood, which deteriorates over time, is being replaced by more practical design and building materials. Other houses are influenced by Thai and Chinese styles, with living quarters upstairs and a shop below. The housing in the northern mountain areas where other ethnic groups (Hmong, Iu Mien, and others) live is geared to withstanding harsh winter weather conditions, built only at ground level and with the roofs sloping downward to reach the ground.

In view of the widespread poverty, many of these houses are modest affairs, with multiple family members occupying them and, in rural areas, livestock being kept underneath the house. The same goes for the houses thrown together next to the river, where there is no sanitation, and many use the river for unsavory purposes as well as depending on it for their livelihood.

There is an alarming disparity between those who live in abject poverty and those who seem to have accumulated huge amounts of wealth through unknown, or certainly administratively unrecorded means, leading the most elite lifestyle. More and more lavish mansions are being built in the capital by wealthy Laotians. While they clearly have access to big money, laborers are on a miserable wage of approximately US $5 per day. The minimum wage is currently LAK 1.1 million per month, which is twenty-six working days— that is, with only Sundays off.

Some private houses have been built in areas where there has been no specific urban planning, architectural framework, or what foreigners consider to be essential infrastructure. As demand grows, serviced apartment blocks are mushrooming in the larger urban areas, many of them catering to foreigners at rates that are completely unaffordable for most locals. As a consequence, landowners and property developers are now reducing the size of the plots to maximize their profit, resulting in high density buildings clustered closely together. There is in fact little implementation or respect for building regulations, and dwellings are often crammed together so tightly that some have rooms with no windows. Satellite dishes blot the horizon everywhere remotely urban, even on the most modest dwellings.

THE HOUSEHOLD

Everyone in the family seems to accept living together, no matter how cramped the conditions. Several generations may cohabit in one house or area, cooking shared meals that are eaten sitting on the floor. If a visitor arrives they are automatically invited to eat as well. Lunches tend to be long, drawn out affairs on hot days.

Family members work together to survive, toiling in the rice paddies, on the river, and helping each other out as best they can. They maintain contact with those relatives who have moved away, and expect them to attend all important occasions such as weddings, births, funerals, or the building of a new house, whenever possible. Neighbors in the community will also always drop in to pay their respects on such occasions.

Family members all contribute to the daily tasks, instinctively understanding the need to support each other in work and all family matters. They also show great respect to the hierarchy of grandparents, always obeying them and being careful not to contradict them. This can be quite an insight for Westerners.

THE *MAEBAN*, HOUSEHOLD HELP

The *maeban*, meaning "mother of the house," is someone who carries out household chores. Up-and-coming Lao families will willingly employ someone, or even a small team of staff, to help them with cooking, cleaning, and caring for children, and such people—often coming from remote rural areas—may live with the family, only going home for specific events.

These modest women, who may speak and read and write in Lao thanks to basic schooling (though many can't read or write well), work hard and show immense respect to their employers with deferential gestures such as bowing and walking backward. Having a *maeban* has become a status symbol among Laotians.

Foreign residents, particularly those with families, would be hard pushed without both a *maeban* and a *nounou,* or nanny. Not only do these people cook and clean and lovingly care for their children, they also shop diligently at the market, translate, handle household bills (written in Lao and generally stuck haphazardly on the gate of the house), and also find other relatives to step in as gardeners, drivers, and so on. Many of them may travel up to twelve miles (20 km) a day on a motorbike to work.

Foreign employers are much more conscious of their employees' welfare, and they may arrange for them to attend English or French classes for better communication—as they generally can't read or write in either of these languages—or cookery classes to help them adapt to Western preferences.

A good *maeban* and her entourage will be passed on from a family who is leaving the country to another, and many are lucky enough to remain in the same house when it is taken on by someone else.

THE LOCAL MARKET

There are many wonderful local markets in Laos, but the village ones may disappoint tourists, as they don't always have picturesque piles of tropical fruit and the like. They may be small, functional affairs, where vendors sell their surplus produce, or even exchange it for other basic items that they need, such as soap, kerosene, medicines, and other less accessible goods. Fruit, vegetables, rice, fish, livestock, wild game, woven clothing, baskets, and even tobacco ... all can be laid out on the ground or on makeshift wooden tables, with or without mats, often in large wicker baskets.

However, with no tourists regularly topping up the economy, these markets give an insight into traditional village and rural life. There is a lively buzz, with women

gossiping, children laughing as they run around and play, buyers carefully scrutinizing—and the occasional foreigner struggling to communicate—so it's great practice for learning the language.

The vendors in Lao villages would rarely think of increasing the price just because their customer is foreign and may have more money, so, unlike the bargaining that everyone is used to in other countries, it is inappropriate and unfair to haggle here. The people of Laos are generally still honest, and are inexperienced in the ways of commerce and trading.

Some villages hold larger markets twice a year in conjunction with religious festivals, when people visit from farther afield and bring handicrafts. These are also occasions when music is played in the evening, albeit from noisy loudspeakers nowadays, but it allows young and old to intermingle and connect.

FAMILY MATTERS
Families in Laos vary as they do everywhere, depending on where they live, their economic and

social standing, and various other factors. What is interesting is that Laos is one of the few countries to retain both a matrilineal and a patrilineal tradition. In some ethnic groups women play an important role in society, in which their lineage is key, and husbands come to live with their families as opposed to the reverse. This is particularly evident among some Lao Loum groups.

However, despite women's dominance in this area, it is men who are looked up to and sought out for the role of village chief, with only minor representation of women's needs in the villages through the Lao Women's Union. And it is men who hold what might be called modern jobs in Laos, and there is clear gender inequality in this area.

Literacy levels are still extremely low in the remote rural areas, with ongoing poverty and malnutrition to contend with in many places throughout the country. Resettlement has started to take a toll on long-standing patterns of mutual family support, in part because people may have lost their traditional livelihood and also because family members are further away from each other because of relocation and alternative housing.

Families are remarkably supportive when it comes to any illness within their ranks, particularly when this entails hospital stays and consultations with doctors and specialists. Someone will be with the patient at all times and, on many occasions, they openly consult and receive information about the patient's condition long before the patients themselves. This is deemed appropriate so that they are not placed under any unnecessary stress. They may travel some distance, and will also ensure that the patient is brought food daily and that someone spends the night by the hospital bed so that they are never alone. At the same time they may well be consulting village healers and making offerings to spirits to improve the patient's prospects.

NAMES AND SURNAMES

The official use of names and surnames in Laos was introduced by the French colonial administration, based on the need to move from oral to written records. It started with the royalty and upper classes and gradually became a national practice. Names in Laos follow the Western order, meaning first the given name followed by the surname. Hmong names often follow the Chinese order—surname followed by given name—but the authorities encourage them to reorder their names to be the same as Lao names. However, there are still many ethnic groups living in remote areas with no surname at all. We have to remember that their language is often not a written one.

Given the linguistic influence of Pali and Sanskrit through the Buddhist scriptures, and the requirements of modern administrative needs, both first names and surnames in Laos are generally a combination of Lao and foreign words. The names reflect a variety of influences, such as nature, animals, astronomy, and royal titles. They can comprise two or three words, containing as many as ten to fifteen letters in English, and it is the Western children attending school in Laos who remember them much more easily than their parents—imagine having to memorize "Soupamoukoune" as a small friend's name! There is also a confusing variety of spellings due to colonial and different linguistic influences. Thus, even the name of a Lan Xang king, Souligna Vongsa, can be seen in non-scholarly journals as Suliyavongsa or Soulignavongsa.

It is still common for people to be called by their first name in Laos, even in formal circumstances, and many people in Laos have nicknames—some derisory, some funny, and others harking back to the past. The latter are based on ancient superstition, being names that ward off evil spirits and keep children healthy and safe. In the past, children in kindergarten would frequently have their names changed if these appeared to be a sign of bad luck. Very few parents are likely to implement this change of name officially, and even now people in Laos still change their names without what Westerners would consider a mandatory administrative procedure.

To foreigners, Lao nicknames can sound rude or silly, but they are generally terms of endearment, and called out in a singsong fashion. Sometimes they indicate the exact opposite of a child's attribute, such as the name Joi, meaning skinny, when they are on the chubby side. They are also based on animals like ducks, mice, or bears (Ped, Mou, Mee). A very common nickname is Pa, which means Fish.

In an academic setting such as a school or university, students may call their teachers by their first names with Mr. or Mrs. in front, such as Mr. Keo or Mrs. Vatsana—one of most popular girls' names, Vatsana means Star. Chanmali (or Chan-malee) means Child of Monday or Born on Monday, following a popular tradition of incorporating the name of the day a child is born into the first name. Other girls' names often heard are Chanthadeth, Phetmany, Bounmy, Sousida, and Malisa.

For boys, anything with Keo (Crystal) is popular as a name, as in Keo, Keophothong, Keophoxai, or Keopersuth. Others are Anoukhon, Anouxay, Tanongsa, Tanonxay, Bounmee, and Bounma. One hears of some first names being used for both boys and girls, depending on the sound of it—for example Chanthavongsa and Keomany. Laotians living abroad tend to have Western first names but middle Lao names. They adapt them to French or English pronunciation.

Common surnames originate from Lao or Laotian (that is, Lao ethnic roots), such as Inthara and Inthavong. "Vong" is a part often added at the end of surnames, and there are two possible explanations for its meaning, one being "family" in Sanskrit and the other indicating royal lineage.

It is also worth noting that Lao people often refer to others by their position in the family rather than by their name. As a foreigner, it can be quite difficult to find out people's real names, even if you spend a lot of time with them. For example, a foreign daughter-in-law may not know what her mother-in-law's name is, as she will always be called "Mother."

EDUCATION

In the old days, education in Laos, as in many other Buddhist countries, was conducted exclusively in monasteries, where monks were trained for years and then went on to offer advice to both the spiritual community and lay people. Due to its culture and ethnic diversity, Laos does not have a long-standing tradition of formal education in public schools.

Education is still free for children who are chosen to become monks or nuns. It is seen as an important opportunity not just for the children, but for their parents too, particularly if they are from rural areas where schooling is very basic. Although public education was officially introduced under French rule in 1893, not only do some villages lack teachers and teaching materials, but sometimes they don't even have a school.

Today, foreign aid and various fundraising efforts are important contributory factors in public education in Laos, as the government has limited funds for this purpose. While plenty of children attend school, distance and accessibility can be a problem, particularly in the rural areas, where the schools are spread out and there is a danger of coming across UXOs left over from the devastating bombing of the Secret War. These children often abandon school at an early age to help their parents work the land or with fishing on the river.

Laos' national educational models have been strongly influenced by both the French and the Anglo-Saxon systems, providing theoretically equal education for all in the country. However, it is proving hard to standardize education with such a wide range of children and backgrounds. Foreign influence has made an impact on education throughout Asia, including Laos, which has several recognized international schools in Vientiane that

ensure stable education for the children of foreign employees. Wealthy Laotians send their children to these schools too, not just because they want to provide them with the best education possible, but because it is perceived as a status symbol. Unlike some private schools that may doctor their exam results, officially recognized international schools must comply with the standard international syllabus and approved exams, and it is very positive for the country to have a growing sector of young multilingual Lao students.

Laos now has eight teacher-training colleges, which is also encouraging. More and more young Laotian students aspire to attend university, and there are branches of the Lao National University in Vientiane opening up in other cities, such as the Souphanouvong University in Luang Prabang, Pakse University, and the University of Savannakhet. Some universities invite visiting foreign academics to give lectures in order to inspire young people in Laos to persevere with their studies and remain in their

country to contribute once qualified. Their interaction with visiting foreign students on placement programs also reveals a whole new prospective world to them.

There are several foreign university programs, fellowships, and scholarships that send students and interns to Laos: PIA (Princeton in Asia), the Fulbright program, French Foreign Ministry initiatives, and others. Many of those are assigned to education services in Laos, such as teaching English as a foreign language or offering specialized medical postgraduate courses (Health Frontiers and others). These latter courses enable vital interaction between local students and international academics, once again in order to motivate the students to gain their degrees, take graduate and postgraduate programs abroad, and ultimately to return home.

The Internet and social media are very popular, and young people in particular all want permanent access, although this may be limited by their location. It has proved to be a positive educational tool, but there are disadvantages, such as inaccurate information sources and the inevitable distractions of social media, live streaming, and the like.

Online Inspiration
A remarkable example of well-utilized Internet is that of a young novice at a temple in Luang Prabang, who taught himself English through watching online videos. He was so inspired by President Obama's speeches about hope and the need for change in Laos that he memorized them by chanting them in the same way as he and his fellow novices did in the temple every day!

TRADITIONAL ENTERTAINMENT

Entertaining generally follows the rhythm of family events: religious ceremonies, marriages, and returns or visits of family members who might have moved away. Money is limited but Laotians are accepting of this. Music plays an important role. One of the most typical Lao traditional musical instruments is the popular *khene* mouth organ, made from bamboo, which even now is used in music and celebrations throughout the land. *Khene/ khaen* mouth organs vary in size and quality of tone, and can have six, sixteen, or eighteen pipes. There is one of eighteen pipes called a *Khaen gao*, which can be up to about six feet (2 m) long. It is played much more rarely nowadays, one of the reasons being that it is too big to be transported on a motorcycle!

The *khene* is an ancient Lao instrument, featuring in many drawings and images. The southern Chinese have confirmed its Lao and Isan origins, but there are similar instruments in the Khmer and Vietnamese traditions, and it is sometimes even attributed to

northern Thailand, China, and Japan. It can be played on its own or with other instruments, such as a flute (*chili akha*) and drum, and even buffalo horns in the past, marking diverse occasions with music and songs for sacred events and rituals honoring spirits (Phi Ban being the spirit who protects villages), the blessing of new home, harvest time, courtship, and marriage. It accompanies the traditional slow round dance between couples, *lamvong*, at festivals. This is the most popular dance in Laos, and is considered a symbol of Lao folk heritage. You will be able to watch it at all major events, and it is particularly important at weddings. You may be invited to join in.

The *khene* also accompanies singers. *Lam* are beautiful chanting songs, with the words improvized on the spur of the moment. The singers sing about the countryside, the beauty of women, or anything that comes to mind and inspires them, and the lyrics are both poetic and romantic.

Other instruments used for accompaniment are gongs, tambourines, flutes, xylophones, string instruments, and bells. There are many opportunities to hear and see wonderful performances, which form an intrinsic part of Laos culture.

In some ethnic groups, such as the Hmong and Akha, the distinction between music for entertainment and ritual music depends on the presence or absence of a sacred instrument. Other people may use the same instrument for different circumstances.

The *khene* has now been enthusiastically taken up by Western musicians, ensuring its continuity with a more modern repertoire of tunes. Sadly, some other traditional Lao instruments are heard less now, and are limited to use in remote villages with ethnic groups such as the Khmou', Oi, Brao, Lao, Phou-noi, Kui, Lolo, Akha, Hmong, and Lantene. People have also got used to the convenience of streaming music from their phones.

chapter **six**

TIME OUT

Life for most working people in Laos is hard, and they
don't have much leisure time. Watching television
is a major pastime, and many workers will describe
their time as being divided between "work, sleep,
and watching television." With such low salaries, it is
difficult to take up pastimes involving any expense.
Although most Lao may be cash-limited, they love
their festivities out on the streets—just join the crowds
to have some fun. You'll be welcomed with courtesy
and a smile. Not only will you enjoy sharing in local
celebrations, particularly when visiting the magnificent
temples, but you'll be moved by the natural beauty of
the country's mountains and rivers.

You can discover lively markets with pyramids of
exotic fruit, savor a cold local beer or sip fresh coconut
water, and sample something from the food stands.
There are excellent new coffee shops opening up,
with innovative menus adapted to Western tastes and
preferences. These new ventures are, of course, designed
for tourists and foreign residents, and are probably
either unknown or completely unaffordable to locals.

FOOD AND DRINK

Lunch, taken with colleagues or friends, has become
an institution in Laos. There is a wide range of options
to suit all tastes and budgets, from basic soup at food

stands to sophisticated menus at foreign restaurants. Cheap labor and weakly enforced taxation have meant that more and more eating places and cafés are springing up all over Vientiane and Luang Prabang.

It's difficult to know where to start or finish in describing all the amazing food traditions of Laos. The cuisine places very strong emphasis on regional and seasonal fresh vegetables, herbs, and spices—chili, coriander, ginger, basil, mint, dill, and garlic. The Lao climate also allows for a wide variety of tropical and seasonal fruits. The Mekong, which in Lao means "the mother of waters," ensures another important ingredient—delicious river fish.

One of the most traditional dishes is *lap* (or *laap*), which is a salad of meat mixed with other, aromatic ingredients. *Lap paa* and *goi paa* are minced fish salads served with fresh vegetables on the side, and typical of southern Laos. Grilled or steamed meats such as pork, chicken, or buffalo are popular choices. Spicy green papaya salad is made from unripe papaya, which tastes more like a vegetable than a fruit.

Soups are also common, based on different vegetables and plants. Try bamboo soup made with fermented fish sauce (*pa daek/paa dek*), a regional specialty.

Noodle dishes have two names, depending on the type of preparation: *feu* (called *pho* in the region) is a noodle soup/broth, and *mee* is a stir-fry. In addition to rice noodles, "cellophane noodles" (also known as "glass noodles") are often used; these are transparent and made from mung bean starch and water.

There are plenty of options for vegetarians, thanks to the local produce that forms part of the Lao staple diet. You can order a dish with tofu (*to-huu*) or with just vegetables (*phak*). Bamboo shoots are added to stews or served as a side dish, and purple banana flowers are also used in salads and other dishes.

Desserts consist of rice too, but this time it's sweet and sticky, and combined with tropical fruits, such as mango (*khao niao mak muang*). There are also drinks, jelly, cream, cakes, and delectable yogurts and ice creams. Cow's milk is a rare commodity, and the locals use very sweet condensed milk in many desserts. Try *khao pard*, a jelly-like rice cake with colored layers, and *khao tom*, steamed rice wrapped in a banana leaf. The French legacy is also still evident in other desserts, plus flans, tarts, and bread. Great baguettes, and other varieties of bread are readily available—even croissants. Street vendors sell sandwiches to locals, not only to Westerners.

The Lao take clever and creative advantage of natural produce for preparation and serving, using banana leaves as bases for grilled food, and bamboo sticks as skewers. They make frequent use of the mortar and pestle, and of woks on charcoal fires, and show extraordinary skill in handling kitchen knives.

Families in Laos often eat together in communal fashion, with food served in *ka toke* style; this is a very low rattan platform used as a table on which to lay out all the different dishes.

Tap water is not safe for drinking, but there is plenty of purified bottled water, sugarcane juices, sodas, coffee, and tea. Fruit and vegetable milkshakes are also popular. There's plenty of beer, of course, and wine is available thanks to the French legacy, with some also being made in Vietnam.

Khao Niao to *Khao Chi*

A dish is not complete without the famous sticky rice, *khao niao*, served in a small bamboo basket. Sticky rice is a Lao staple—a glutinous rice that is rolled into balls. Because of its consistency it's best eaten by hand, and you can dip it into the sauce on your plate or ask for a *jeow,* a spicy homemade tomato, eggplant, or mushroom sauce, or a sweet peanut sauce. It can also be served on bamboo sticks, making the whole process easier and less sticky on the hands. Occasionally, there are basins for handwashing in the central area of the restaurant—unusual but very useful! Sticky rice coated with eggs and grilled is a very popular snack found on carts all over the city nowadays.

Khao chi is the Lao word for wheat-based bread, which is a French-inspired legacy.

Unreadable Menus, Delicious Food
There are no menus at food stalls, as you can imagine, so your choices will have to be based on recommendation or go by appearance and smell. In local restaurants, menus may be handwritten in white chalk on blackboards, scribbled on a piece of paper, or, occasionally, printed. They may only be written in Lao, or if translated can be unreliable or hilarious— examples include intriguing options such as "prawn cutie" or "prawn with fist sauce." In Vientiane, a rice noodle soup, *foe,* is generally available at any time in restaurants.

For the more adventurous, sample some of the lesser-known delicacies eaten by locals, such as grilled grasshopper (described as "crunchy but nutritious" by Westerners), or small fried birds of different species with such fine bones that they are simply impossible to remove—so chomp up, and down the hatch! Fried toads, beetles, worms, and even dragonflies are more popular crunchy snacks. Fried mulberry leaves are another tasty and unusual vegetarian option, freshly picked, fried in piping hot oil, and eaten at once with a honey and lemon dip.

Eating an egg containing a chick after it has been incubated for almost three weeks is considered to be an extremely useful source of protein (*khai look*).

Coffee Culture

Coffee was first planted during the French period between 1913 and 1916, with many different varieties brought from the botanical gardens in Saigon. Tradition says that it was first planted in the small village of Thateng, in the northern part of the Bolaven Plateau. Today, coffee is one of the top income earners among Laos' agricultural exports and its fifth-most important export product. Most goes to Taiwan, Thailand, Vietnam, and Japan. Coffee is exported to the US as well, and to Europe—Italy, Spain, Poland, Germany, France, Belgium, and Sweden.

With the perfect geology and climate for coffee cultivation, the Bolaven Plateau produces excellent coffee beans. Thirty miles (50 km) wide, and 3,280 feet (1,000 m) above sea level, it is located in the warmer, southern part of Laos. The combination of a wet but cool microclimate, lush jungle vegetation, iron-rich volcanic soil, and plentiful water supply makes for perfect shade-grown coffee. Tea is also grown, and many families living in the villages scattered around the plateau are sustained through work at these plantations. This area has stunning waterfalls.

The emerging coffee culture combines Western and Lao coffee traditions, with lots of different recipes. Locals like their coffee thick and very sweet, made with condensed milk. Iced coffee is long and cooling. Gourmet cafés in the cities take great pride in employing well-trained *baristas*, with courses available for anyone wanting to learn.

Coffee has become a great new way of promoting tourism in Laos, so in 2014 the first Lao Coffee Festival was held in the Pakse district of the province of Champasak. Likewise, organic production of both tea and coffee is becoming increasingly popular with both producers and customers, although the authenticity of the "organic" claim can be dubious, with no set regulations established in the country as yet.

Beer

Lao beer has become a national institution, and there is a fair amount of national overindulgence too! The Beerlao company was founded in 1973 as a joint Franco–Lao venture, but was then nationalized in 1975 with the establishment of Lao PDR. It has since expanded hugely, and is co-owned by the Lao government and Carlsberg Group, also producing soft drinks. The brewery is on the outskirts of Vientiane, and employs over 700 staff.

Three types of beer are produced under the iconic Beerlao brand: Beerlao Lager, Beerlao Gold, and Beerlao Dark. In Laos beer is drunk with ice, which is a bit of a shock to dedicated Western beer drinkers—but you soon get to like it in the heat! Foreign beers are now available to meet tourist demand, costing up to US $8–10 a bottle—quite a price, when you consider that some locals survive on that amount for a whole week.

SHOPPING

There is a great variety of shopping possibilities for people living in or visiting Laos, with many Western products readily available from Thai supermarkets and shopping malls in the border towns.

Local country markets provide all sort of products and services aside from the standard fruit, vegetables, fish, meat, herbs, coffee, and tea. You will see baskets laden with grasshoppers and other insects, and even small wild game and birds for sale. Practical items such as school stationery, hardware, haberdashery, and

electrical goods can be found, and some stands offer hand sewing repairs or custom-made clothing. Others make up flags from any country of your choice.

There is generally a wide range of souvenirs and handicrafts from local and regional sources. Wood carvings of Buddhist-related objects are very popular.

Craftsmen also make different statues, masks, and candleholders at the main markets in Vientiane and

"We Bought a House in Laos"

An Australian friend sent us a message with the heading "We bought a house in Laos," and we were very excited but intrigued too! Everyone is aware that foreigners cannot own property in Laos unless they "team up" with a Lao citizen, in whose name it would have to be registered, and this is not the sort of information that you would openly share. We also knew that our friends were leaving this beautiful country in a matter of weeks—so how had they managed it? Just as we were conjuring up a vision of visiting them in their new home, up popped a photo of a brightly colored miniature plaster house, and the rest of the message read: "It's a Spirit House!" One should treat such cultural and spiritual purchases with extreme sensitivity to avoid giving offense.

Our friends had organized professional transportation of all their belongings to their next destination, so they added a Spirit House weighing several hundred kilos to bring back happy memories of Laos. These exquisite miniature houses come in many different sizes. They may be made of wood, and transported in flat-pack kit form.

Luang Prabang, and it is well worth watching them at work. There are a few antique shops, but beware of so-called antique carvings, which may or may not be genuine, or could even be stolen from temples.

People in Laos like silver jewelry, and bracelets with different motifs—flowers, butterflies, and dragonflies—as well as gold. Westerners may be disconcerted by the recent trend to create jewelry from recovered UXO from the Secret War.

Some markets specialize in artisan items, such as pottery and jewelry. Woven wicker baskets, panniers, and mats are a great buy. Visit the village workshops to watch the womenfolk weaving and dyeing cotton and silk. The designs are based on Lao folklore, Buddhist symbols, and the natural environment. In Laos, dragons are the symbol for prestige and protection. There are many different articles of clothing, and shawls, throws, and rugs that will remind you of their makers' extraordinary talents when you are back home.

Shimmering Silks and Handy Baskets

Visitors go wild for the stunning silk weave garments available at the market for a fraction of the prices they are elsewhere. The designs and colors are gorgeous, and they are mostly woven by local women at home.

Bamboo and rattan baskets are hugely popular and come in all shapes and sizes for multiple uses—shopping, as a lunch box, for steaming, and, for foreigners, as lovely lightweight objects to take home. The green backpack baskets might be tricky, but the people of Laos have relied on these for a very long time! Many of these baskets are still used by all ethnic groups, but with a variation of style in accordance with the tradition of the many different hill tribe villages. They are truly authentic and intricately woven, mostly by men. Depending on each artist and the basket's use, they can be plain and functional or complex and decorative.

NIGHTLIFE

Don't expect crazy nightlife in Laos, and remember that for years this kind of activity was completely frowned upon and restricted. The pace for visitors is more laid back, with relaxed riverside venues for drinking and dining out. Vientiane has just a handful of nightclubs, and they close around midnight. There might be live music and a dance floor in some of the local bars.

Laotians are also really fond of karaoke, and have loudspeakers to publicize it at many organized venues, as well as separate impromptu portable ones in other areas, so that you can be hit by a cacophony of different music all at once!

FILM FESTIVALS

Laos is now an active participant in the Southeast Asian film world, and this is a medium that is quietly promoting the diversity of Lao culture and putting the country on the map. It also opening up the world to Lao people, who are not used to watching movies, and in addition enabling them to view the scenery and drama of their own country in film format. However, not all the films that are made in Laos are actually allowed to be shown in the country. Film festivals are held annually in Luang Prabang and Vientiane.

Chang—a Documentary Drama Made in 1927

This amazing silent documentary was actually filmed in a remote area in the northern Thai province of Nan, then Siam (on a budget equivalent today to US $60), but could easily depict Laos in olden times. Based on the story of a Lao tribesman's fight to protect his meager livestock from the wild beasts of the jungle, even now it provides deep insight into the trials and tribulations of man and beast (*chang/xang* meaning elephant) and the need to learn to respect each other in order to coexist. The filming is very realistic, with many of the objects and daily activities still existing after all these years, such as the making of woven baby-baskets and rice panniers, and the traditional growing of crops and rearing of animals.

SPORTS AND GAMES

Sports have long been part of both ritual and recreational life in Laos. The That Luang festival has always included a traditional game of field hockey, played with bamboo sticks, although sadly this is no longer so common.

Laos is not known for sport on an international level, and has never won an Olympic medal or participated in the Winter Olympics. However, it was one of the founding countries of the Southeast Asian Games (SEA) in 1959, and hosted them in 2009. You may see promo T-shirts blazoning logos such as Laos–SEA – nothing to do with the seaside, which the country doesn't have, of course!

Soccer (football) is the most popular national sport these days, and Laos has a national team that was founded in 1951. Rugby is also popular, and is played by both men and women from the Lao Rugby Federation.

Not to be dismissed are the country's traditional sports, such as *kator*, a mixture of volleyball and football, played with a rattan ball by players using their feet instead of

their hands to get the ball over the net. *Tikhi* is a traditional game resembling field hockey.

Muay Lao are popular martial arts practiced in Laos, similar to kick-boxing in Thailand. *Muay Thai*, an extreme form of unarmed combat, is practiced by Lao refugees in Thailand.

Sports are promoted in Laos' rural and urban areas, with local regional and national competitions taking place, drawing people together on an important and enjoyable social basis. Visitors cannot fail to enjoy the buzz as well.

Further attractions are the annual sporting events and festivals. Don't miss the famous dragon boat racing known as *Buon Suang Heua*, held at various locations in Laos and drawing in large crowds of spectators (see page 71).

OUTDOOR ACTIVITIES

There is great potential for rural tourism and ecotourism in Laos, and this includes activity holidays offering trekking, cycling, climbing, ziplining, camping, and other outdoor pursuits. These seem to be particularly popular with South Korean tourists— impossible to miss in large color-coordinated groups in the National Parks. However, despite the fact that Laos boasts twenty National Protected Areas covering almost 14 percent of the country, not all of them are accessible to the public. The Phou Khao Khouay area with its stunning waterfalls lies close to the capital, and now has camping facilities for visitors (rent a tent on-site).

VISITING A TEMPLE

There is something very special about observing, and even participating in, the religious and spiritual ceremonies in the many wonderful temples in Laos. Buddhist monks used to be persecuted, but now this predominant faith seem to have regained much of its former official approval and once again the temples are centers of solemn worship, activity, and learning.

There are a myriad temples to be visited, from the UNESCO-listed Wat Phou in Southern Laos, to Wat Sisaket in Vientiane, and the emblematic sixteenth-century Wat Xieng Thong in Luang Prabang.

Many visitors come to Laos to switch off from their modern technological world, and here they can enjoy the benefits of yoga and meditation in beautiful sacred surroundings. Several of the temples in Vientiane hold weekly meditations that everyone is welcome to join, with chanting as well as walking in silence around the temple grounds. There is a great sense of spirituality, benevolence, and harmony as many nationalities join together.

As in all religious places, it is essential to show respect when visiting the temples. On no account should a woman touch a monk or his robes. It is also important that you do not touch sacred items or enter sacred sites without permission. In many places it is customary to leave a small donation after your visit.

You will see that not all the temples are well conserved, with some losing their surrounding areas to car-parking spaces.

SOME CULTURAL MUST-SEES
Luang Prabang—Culture and Nature Combined
The ancient royal city and heart of Laos, Luang Prabang is a UNESCO world heritage site. It is full of historic temples, all within easy walking distance. Visitors can also actively participate in some of the morning or evening ceremonies, *Tak Bat*, morning alms-giving, being the most popular. Already this lovely city is undergoing change because of growing tourism and other industries, with a great deal of alterations to some buildings.

Vientiane
This small and graceful capital city still reflects the French colonial era in its houses and buildings. It also

has some of the most revered temples in Laos, such as
the Haw Phra Kaew and the Wat Sisaket. The Pha That
Luang, the great golden stupa situated on a hill, was
originally built in 1566, but entirely destroyed. What we
see today is a reconstruction built by the French in the
1930s, based on ancient drawings. It is the symbol of
Vientiane as well as of the Buddhist religion, and is said
to contain a sacred relic from the Buddha.

Buddha Park, or Xieng Khuan

This amazing sculpture park is on the Mekong River,
about sixteen miles (25 km) outside Vientiane and
past the Friendship Bridge. It contains a collection of
hundreds of Buddhist and Hindu statues scattered
around a meadow. It was built in 1958 by the monk
Bunleua Sulilat and his students, all untrained artists.
Some of the statues impress by their sheer size, such as
an enormous reclining Buddha.

Wat Phou—Ancient Khmer Temple Complex

Located at the foot of a sacred mountain, this set
of temple remains blends perfectly with the natural
environment. Climb the centuries-old stone staircase

under frangipani trees that seem to grow directly out of the rock. It is located in Champasak Province in southern Laos and is listed as a UNESCO World Heritage Site.

The Plain of Jars (Thong Hai Hin or Thong Haihin)

This famous site has also been proposed as a UNESCO World Heritage Site. Located south of Phonsavan, 217 miles (350 km) by road from Vientiane in Xiangkhouang Province, it lies between 200 and 3,900 feet (between 1,000 and 1,200 meters) above sea level.

The huge stone jars are sculpted from sandstone rock, and weigh several hundred tons. Their sizes vary, with some over 9 feet (3 m) high, and they are empty. Their purpose is not clear, although there are various local legends, and archaeologists suggest that they might have been used as urns in burial rituals.

Other Places of Interest

Viengxai Caves

These caves, located in Hua Phan Province, next to the Vietnamese border, were home to 20,000 Pathet Lao soldiers during the Indochina conflict.

Cooperative Orthotic and Prosthetic Enterprise

This cooperative (COPE) is a visitor and rehabilitation center in Vientiane that makes prosthetic limbs for people injured by UXO. It also has a museum dedicated to explaining the devastating effects of uncleared UXO.

SITES OF NATURAL BEAUTY

You need time to enjoy Laos fully, particularly when it comes to visiting its natural beauty sites. Don't be deceived by distance measured in miles and GPS ETA calculation Apps. Everything will take a bit longer off the beaten path, and the best approach is to relax and enjoy the experience. A good motto in Laos is "If you are in a hurry, you're in the wrong country."

Remember that hills and mountains account for 70 percent of the landmass. While there are many rivers, Laos has few lakes and reservoirs.

Discovering Laos by River

Seeing Laos from the water is an essential part of your trip, and there are various ways of doing this on all the navigable parts of the great Mekong River. Day trips on slow boats (Luang Prabang to just north of Nhong Kiaw being one), kayaks, dragon boats, and the like are all great options, but if you have the time take one of the two- to three-day cruises.

Wow Factor Waterfalls

There are many waterfalls in Laos, including the largest waterfall in Southeast Asia, Kohne Phapheng Falls, in Champasak Province in the south.

Hike Through Fantastical Rock Formations

Ninety-three miles (150 km) north of Vientiane lies Van Vieng, a natural playground of soaring limestone mountains, caves, waterfalls, and lagoons. Rent a motorcycle for a day to explore the traditional villages and rice paddies, and discover the amazing karst landscape and spectacular views. There is hiking, climbing, caving, canyoning, rafting, ziplining, and hot-air ballooning.

Canyons and Caves: Kong Lor

Kong Lor Cave is a limestone cave in the Phu Hin Bun National Park in Khammouane Province, north of Thakhek and accessible on a long, dusty dirt track through huge tropical trees. Boat transport to the caves is organized from the village with the same name. This is one of the world's longest navigable caves at 4.7 miles (7.5 km), and long-tail boats take you through an underground section of the Hin Boun River.

Si Phan Don, the Mekong River Archipelago
Down in the south of Laos, this small and utterly peaceful archipelago consists of no fewer than 4,000 islets in the heart of the Mekong as it meanders on to Cambodia and the Tonle Sap lake. It is an ideal place to relax. The freshwater dolphins are high on everyone's list.

Loop Around the Bolaven Plateau on a Motorcycle
Rent your motorcycle in Pakse in southern Laos and be sure to take a map! This is a lovely two-day trip, where you'll discover remote rural areas with beautiful landscapes, charming villages, and waterfalls.

Don Daeng
This sandy river island, five miles (8 km) long, is a hidden treasure with a great laid-back feel. A visit can be combined with the Wat Phou temple complex from Champasak. Its community accommodation and homestays are genuine experiences.

Visiting Villages in Northern Laos
A variety of ethnic tribes live here in harsh, mountainous weather conditions. Their traditions have barely changed as they struggle to survive, close to the source of the Mekong River.

Ecotourism is another growing industry, and the government is becoming more aware of the need to protect the country's fragile biodiversity.

chapter seven

TRAVEL, HEALTH, & SAFETY

As so much of Laos is mountainous and the road network is poorly developed, flying is by far the most efficient way of getting around. However, if you have the time, traveling within the country overland, or from Thailand to Laos by boat, is an enriching experience and a wonderful way to enjoy the scenery and culture.

ARRIVING

Many countries in the region are a good gateway into Laos. There are plenty of daily flights from Thailand, Vietnam, Cambodia, Myanmar, China, South Korea, and Japan. Bangkok is a real hub for Laos, with direct day and sleeper train connections to towns in northern Thailand such as Chiang Mai and Nong Khai, from where it is easy to reach Laos. There are several boat crossings, including a slow boat from Thailand.

There are no direct flights between Europe and Laos. The national company Lao Airlines operates most internal flights, in addition to international services to China, Thailand, Vietnam, Cambodia, and Singapore. There are also several low-cost airlines in the region (such as Tigerair, AirAsia, and Nok).

Border crossings can be frustrating, with excessive administrative procedures and an alarming number of officers in uniform—a lingering legacy of the totalitarian regime that tends to make travelers uneasy. The crossing points vary in their vigilance and procedure, and frequent travelers are used to good and bad days within the same week. Foreigners who have settled in Vientiane frequently cross the border, on weekly shopping trips or to get to the airport, Udon Thani, and have simply had to get used to the situation. Border crossings are closed at night, but will generally be opened for an urgent reason, such as a medical emergency.

Visas

Visas are available on arrival at several (but not all, so be sure to check) land or air borders. The application fee has to be paid in cash, in kip, US dollars, or Thai baht. The visa fee is determined by nationality, but for most countries this costs US $30–42. Tourist visas can be renewed in Vientiane, for US $2 a day, but the fee is increased to $10 a day once visitors exceed their stay. Regulations frequently change everywhere in Asia, and Laos is used for "visa runs," when travelers whose visas for neighboring countries have expired and they have to leave that country in order to reapply for a new visa and return. Business visas are explained on page 146.

Crossing the Border by Car

This can be quite a procedure. Fees vary: technically you are exporting and reimporting your car from one country to the next, even for a day crossing, and you must pay each trip. The Thai authorities are much more vigilant about car insurance documents than those in Laos.

There are also questionable on-the-spot extra fees extracted from unwitting travelers, some for incomprehensible reasons such as "temperature checking" or reexamining your visa. They are small amounts—maybe 8,000 kip (about US $1). Foreigners tend to pay these rather than risk additional demands.

Currency
The local currency is the Lao kip. There is a maximum withdrawal at ATMs in Laos of about US $200, with an additional ATM fee of US $5–10, plus international bank charges for foreign transactions.

GETTING AROUND
By Air
The first Lao airports were built by the French, many for military rather than civilian use. However, with more foreign demand and financial assistance, the network has gradually expanded. There are five international airports: Vientiane, Luang Prabang, Pakse (flights to Siem Reap), Savannakhet (flights to BKK), and Attapeu (which currently has no flights to anywhere). These are not much used by local people.

By Road
In Town
Public transportation consists of buses, open *tuk-tuks* that stop anywhere when hailed, and taxis. The taxis are not metered, and fares must be agreed in advance.

Long-Distance Buses
Approximately 80 percent of roads in Laos are just dirt tracks, although most of those leading into main towns have been properly surfaced. In this long,

narrow, north–south country, the principal route is, of course, north–south. There are various options, including overnight buses with sleeper-type cubicles and a hop-on/hop-off system all the way. Be warned that the Lao are unaware of the Western procedure of standing in line when it comes to purchasing tickets or boarding a bus! Bus services can be erratic and painfully slow, but people on board will be friendly, despite the language barrier.

By Car

Despite the potholes, car journeys should be treated as an adventure and a chance to immerse oneself in everyday life in Laos. This does, of course, entail the possibility of infractions and accidents, which apparently can be dealt with in an unconventional manner by some officials—that is, you pay a small "fee," and a police report miraculously vanishes into thin air. Many foreigners now take the precaution of recording their driving to have evidence in case of an accident, using a small camera, mounted on the inside of the windshield, that films their whole journey.

Cars with a driver can be provided, but it is possible to rent a car and drive on your own. Many of the international car hire companies operate in Laos. Don't rely on GPS as it is not updated regularly enough, and many dirt roads are not marked at all, but do go, if you leave enough time—adventure awaits!

Speed limits do not apply because one can't drive faster than the potholes allow.

Two Wheels

Bus services can be erratic and painfully slow, so a great way to get around and explore is by motorbike. The roads will be bumpy and dusty, but you'll be a lot more independent and open to new experiences.

The main motorbike brand is Kolao, a joint venture between Korea and Laos (hence the name), and they are easy to rent or buy. There are several popular motorbike trips and loops around Laos, with the Ho Chi Min Trail high up on the must-do list. You'll need a valid motorcycle license for insurance purposes.

Punctures are a regular occurrence, given the potholes, and you may well encounter a few other mechanical issues as well. But don't despair; help is at hand. Keep an eye out for piles of spare tires on the sidewalk or hanging from the ceiling in small roadside shops. There's often just a minimal repair charge, by Western standards. There are plenty of Kolao spare parts available, and repairs are possible on virtually every street corner.

Don't attempt to emulate the local custom of overloading your bike with other people, babies, livestock, and provisions!

By Boat

There are pleasure trips and cruises for tourists, and slow boats and larger ferries used by local people.

WHERE TO STAY

Accommodation in Laos covers most preferences and budgets, ranging from simple hostels and rooms to high-end boutique hotels. The Internet has revolutionized advertising, and there are more than 300 private accommodation options listed on different Web sites by eager property owners—but proceed cautiously, as there is no government regulation. Remember that quality as well as prices and services can vary significantly in this country, and that there is virtually no regulation or enforcement of standards of hospitality services. However, the Lao people are genuine and honest for the most part, and there is a certain element of charm to this simple approach to hospitality, as opposed to the ever-growing regulations needed to meet the demands of foreign visitors in other countries that have so radically changed the holiday landscape.

Hotel rooms cost anything between US $20 and US $400 a night, and sometimes more. Guesthouses are usually small, and are more economical, with prices starting at US $4 a night. There are also lodges that can be located in natural surroundings, near a waterfall or a river. Another interesting experience is a family home-stay. If you choose this option it is worth remembering that sanitation facilities will be very basic, and certainly not what you are used to.

When it comes to seeking accommodation at special events in remote towns, such as the famous two-day Xayabouri Elephant Festival way north of Vientiane, friends, family, and foreign visitors are squeezed in everywhere (even on mattresses in a corridor) over this brief and fun period.

Another great way of immersing yourself in local life is to stay at a "community guesthouse," where you rent a room from families who have jointly built guesthouses in their village, and your food is brought by different families on different days. A good example is on the Mekong island of Don Deng, in a great location with wonderful views of the dunes and amazing locally prepared food fresh from the river.

It is customary for any foreigner wishing to spend time in a private home in an urban area or rural village to inform the local village chief, or *nai ban*, of their presence. One's stay used to be very closely monitored, but these days there is a financial interest, whereby a contributory tax is levied on paying guests.

Renting Long-Term

Visitors intending to stay for a longer period must pay at least six months' or even a year's rent up front, often in cash, and directly to the owner. This will be within a somewhat limited legal framework, but foreigners often have no option but to accept.

HEALTH

Nominally there is free national health coverage, but in practice the government facilities are under resourced, as funds may end up in private hands. Traditional medicine is widely popular and more affordable. Although there are many pharmacies, the branded products they stock may not be genuine.

Health experts have expressed concern about safe water, sanitation, and hygiene in many rural and some urban areas. All visitors should take standard hygiene precautions, particularly with regard to drinking clean water from clean containers and washing your hands frequently with soap and water to avoid contamination or infection. Bottled water is readily available.

Vaccinations

Although the only obligatory vaccination is against yellow fever if you have visited affected areas, the main threat is generated by all mosquito-borne and other tropical diseases (malaria, dengue, zika, chikungunya, Japanese encephalitis). Be sure to check on all relevant vaccinations before traveling. Nevertheless, Laos does not generally suffer from massive outbreaks of tropical diseases. What is important is that you seek medical attention at once if you show any of the classic symptoms.

Hospitals and Clinics
Unfortunately, the quality of medicine in local hospitals in Laos is still way off what Westerners expect, and also depends on where you are in the country. Equipment is basic and practice is substandard, with no oversight on the government's part. However, there are foreign clinics in Vientiane, such as the Alliance International Medical Center ("Thai Clinic") and the French Embassy Medical Center ("French Clinic").

For more serious emergencies and surgical operations, the safest option is to cross the Mekong River and go to one of the hospitals in Thailand in the border towns that are accessible by car, such as Nongkhai (Wattana Hospital), Udon Thani (AEK International Hospital), or, if time permits, Bangkok, which some prefer.

When going by car, bear in mind that bridge crossing schedules can change and some may even be closed at night. However, there are certain agreements between the emergency transport services in Laos and the hospitals in Thailand, allowing the opening of a bridge in special circumstances. It may come at a price, or through a person with good connections who is willing to help.

SAFETY

Laos is still a very safe place—considerably safer than the neighboring countries. The only security guards tend to be outside official buildings and embassies, and there are no gated communities. Nevertheless, commonsense precautions apply. Stay vigilant and look after yourself and your personal effects. Watch out for petty thieves, and don't expose yourself to unnecessary risk.

Be wary when driving, especially on poor or virtually nonexistent roads and tracks in rural areas, or in the chaotic traffic conditions of the urban areas, where many disregard traffic regulations. Avoid driving at night in unfamiliar areas if possible. Check your insurance if you rent a car or motorbike, as in the case of an accident you may have to pay out on damaged tires or vehicle repairs. The police have been known to expect a "small fee" to waive an infraction, and even confiscate the passports of unwitting foreigners until the financial side is resolved. Don't ever leave your ID with the rental company.

And, finally, be respectful of weather conditions— you probably don't get monsoons where you come from! Temperature differences can be extreme, particularly in the mountains, so ensure you have the right clothing with you.

Take Photos, but Take Care

Don't take photos of any military buildings or installations, or indeed anything that may be sensitive to national security or evidence of unofficial practices. You don't want to be hauled into a police station and interrogated, or have your phone or camera confiscated.

chapter eight

BUSINESS BRIEFING

THE BUSINESS ENVIRONMENT

In Laos there are clear economic openings, even if tight control over the political space still exists. Lao PDR's economic boom is driven primarily by foreign direct investment in natural resource extraction and hydropower. Attempting to ensure that this is conducted in an environmentally sustainable way, and that the revenues generated benefit everyone, is critical for the development of the country.

There are already many construction projects going on in Vientiane as well as in Pakse and other cities. The majority of this construction is for commercial purposes, such as shops, hotels, and offices for visitors from outside Laos. Other new projects are designed to meet the growing demand for accommodation by the expatriate community living and working in the country

ASEM and ASEAN Summits

Vientiane hosted the 2012 ASEM (Asia–Europe Meeting) summit, which initiated the construction of the Vientiane New World (VNW) mega project, including a big luxury housing complex located in the center of Vientiane by the Mekong River and not far from the Presidential Palace. There was a small fishing village on the site, and the inhabitants were resettled elsewhere. Leaders, government heads, and senior officers from forty-six countries all stayed there during the ninth ASEM Summit.

When President Obama attended the ASEAN (Association of Southeast Asian Nations) summit in 2016, during Laos' presidency of the association, his speech met with mixed reviews, but one strong message was the following: "We believe that there needs to be good governance, because people should not have to pay a bribe to start a business or sell their goods." There are other concerns yet to be overcome. Despite improvement over the past few years, public debt is high and the economy is still vulnerable.

Over the last thirty years, Laos has made slow but steady progress in implementing reforms and building the institutions necessary for a functioning market economy. Major trading partners include Thailand, China, and Vietnam. The main exports are timber, mining commodities, and hydroelectricity. Major imports include machinery, equipment, and motor vehicles. Economic development has led to a rising tide of disputes over land and environmental issues with many foreign-owned mining, logging, and farming concessions.

Implications and Consequences of ASEAN

Laos is one of ten members of ASEAN, which, with the exception of China, represents the second-largest group of trading partners outside Europe, and has about 640 million consumers.

ASEAN has had a direct impact on the flow of trade throughout Asia. It has created huge growth in global manufacturing and supply, particularly since the trade agreements established with China and India in 2010. Bilateral trade between China and the Big Five of ASEAN (Indonesia, Malaysia, Philippines, Singapore, and Thailand) has risen by 500 percent since 2010, while the smaller ASEAN countries such as Cambodia, Laos, Myanmar, and Vietnam (CLMV) are also gradually complying with customs duty reductions. Import and export tariffs are close to zero for many products, including the massive consumer markets in China and India with a combined total of 500 million middle-class consumers.

There is also the establishment and development of Special and Specific Economic Zones (SEZs) within Laos, which will need to be carefully managed. The SEZs allow for a relaxation of the government's economic policies and greater flexibility in specific areas. On the other hand, villagers who are relocated to make way for the SEZ developments may be unable to have access to new means of livelihood.

Laos served as the chair of ASEAN in 2016. It held the main ASEAN meeting, but did not host a meeting of ASEAN civil society groups as part of its chairmanship. Generally, the EU cooperates with ASEAN, holding regular meetings and discussions regarding trade and investment at the ministerial and official senior economic level. As Laos falls into the category of Least Developed Country (LDC), it reaps great benefits through the EU's economy-based Everything But Arms (EBA) scheme.

From Landlocked to Landlinked

After years of isolation, Laos is opening up. The new hi-tech railway running from the Chinese province of Yunnan will link Laos with several countries and seaports, benefiting many passengers and companies moving freight. There will be further development of the seaports in both Vietnam and Cambodia, in addition to Thailand's Laem Chabang deep sea port, which is 416 miles (670 km) south of Vientiane.

The Laos economy is driven mainly by hydropower, as well as by mining and natural resources, construction, real estate, and tourism services. Establishing a railway network should boost many of those activities. In the Trans-Asian Railway network, the missing link—filling an important gap via Laos—is expected to be in operation by late 2021, turning the landlocked communist state into what Lao officials are enthusiastically calling a "landlinked" country. All of this cannot fail to boost economic growth. However, the flat land on each side of the track will be expropriated from its owners.

BUSINESS ETIQUETTE AND PROTOCOL

As until recently Laos was cut off by what was known as the "bamboo curtain," the Lao people have gleaned their knowledge of—and gradually developed—modern-style business management, technological devices, protocol, and behavior by observing the business practices of other Asian countries. They already had some prior knowledge of European protocol thanks to the French colonial influence, but these days there is greater awareness of American, Australian, and indeed Chinese business styles.

Many more business initiatives are being introduced into Laos than are originating there. It is an important challenge for Laotians to understand and adapt to this new professional environment.

In the office coworkers may greet their colleagues with the typical Asian *nop*, which has made a comeback. (See page 81.) Shaking hands is now widely practiced as well in places like Vientiane, by both men and women. Management staff will be greeted with more attention, with female coworkers feeling bound to do a *nop* whenever a senior person passes by. The normal social etiquette of hierarchy, age, and seniority is reflected in the office environment.

An open-door policy is rarely applied among local management staff, and standard office regulations and protocol can be strict.

Foreigners may be surprised to find that people are often called by their first name, even in some formal settings. Lao people may be addressed by their first names, but preceded by their title "Mrs. /Mr.," or the title "Than," followed by their first name if they occupy a position of respect.

Dress Code
The office dress code is a vibrant mix of Asian and Western. Many Western women will proudly wear their locally made *sinh* skirts, but with a Western top. Asian women will more frequently choose a classically sewn silk or cotton top. For men, full business suits are required only for official meetings, while more casual long-sleeved shirts, with or without a tie or jacket, are widely accepted.

SETTING UP A MEETING

Some advance planning can be very useful. First, have a business card printed in both English and Lao to present at an initial meeting.

English is becoming more widely spoken, despite the fact that many senior government officials are fluent in French. However, foreigners should always enquire whether their business partner is fluent in English. Otherwise, employ an interpreter to ensure a smooth meeting and follow-up. A reliable interpreter could be an important asset for a company. Chinese companies often bring along Chinese linguists who are studying the Lao language back in China, thus avoiding any cultural misunderstandings in terms of important business decisions from the start.

When setting up a meeting, correspondence and communication should be addressed to the senior decision-makers. Decisions often take a considerable length of time as they are relayed up and down the chain of hierarchy due to the omnipresent lack of delegation within companies or government ministries. It used to be virtually impossible to reach anyone of authority on a landline phone number. Most senior executives today have several cell phone numbers, and even though the main cell phone number might be the one their secretary uses, all of the most important business partners will be given direct cell phone access to their senior counterpart.

PRESENTATIONS

Good audiovisual aids are essential, as computer presentations are part of every formal business presentation these days. Local staff will rarely ask questions but will listen quietly instead and, in the big lecture halls, you may spot them using their cell phones—like many others, attempting to multitask.

Be warned that when speaking a foreign language to the people of Laos there may be misunderstandings, as people frequently reply with a "yes" to direct questions, but only as an acknowledgement, and not necessarily grasping what you have said at all!

Leave time for questions and answers at the end, but remember that people may be inhibited about asking sensitive questions as, given the presence of new technology, sessions may end up online.

NEGOTIATIONS

It is essential to determine the hierarchy and seniority of the people in any business dealings at the outset, and identify those responsible for decision-making. Bargaining is expected in most commercial transactions, and although Lao people are generally polite and gentle hagglers, they are persistent.

Bear in mind that some of those present may be offered inducements by the organizing authority. As government salaries are low, the *per diem* and travel allowances paid to local staff for participation in training, including attending meetings, is considered significant and might influence the choice of attendees.

Negotiations may be long and confusing, direct questions may never be answered by potential Lao business partners, and agreements may not be honored. Government laws and regulations are another challenge, being opaque and subject to change. Be advised: investing in Laos is not for amateurs.

BUREAUCRACY

Bureaucracy still complicates life in Laos, and one of the main reasons is that the government has yet to come to grips with the processes needed to deal with a growing economy and foreign investment. There are plenty of new laws and taxes, but that doesn't mean that they are applied or dealt with in a consistent or speedy manner. Very little is translated into any foreign language, which can make matters difficult as there are no officially qualified translators or interpreters. The use of the Internet and electronic administration is limited, and many locals still rely on word of mouth for information. They also tend to come across as having a casual business approach.

As a result, foreigners in particular are overwhelmed by the complexity of a combination of informal agreements, new laws and taxes, and permits, and the constant need to provide the same documentation again and again. They are often poorly advised, only to find that they may face sanctions. However, all of these issues are slowly starting to change and improve.

PERMITS AND ADMINISTRATION

There are different ways, both formal and informal, to obtain work and residence permits. Today, for the payment of a specific fee, there is often an alternative method of being granted a "small business working permit" for one year.

Another important issue for foreigners is whether or not they can legally buy and register land in their own name. They cannot. There are other ways of obtaining property, such as through "joint venture" land ownership with locals, through business deals, or by marriage, but these are not without risk. Also, in some cases the state will requisition land with minimal or no compensation.

Administrative matters related to foreign employees working in the private and public sectors, as well as in NGOs, are regulated by the 2013 Labor Law. The Ministry of Labor and Social Affairs issues work permits, while residence permits are issued by the Immigration Department at the Ministry of Public Security. Most work permits are issued for one year, and are renewable for up to five years. Extensions beyond that time are exceptional, and rare. Despite seemingly clearly defined sections detailing the conditions and documents needed in order to be employed in Lao PDR, the last condition contradicts it all completely, specifying that a foreign worker must comply with "other conditions as deemed necessary"!

There are three types of working visa for foreigners planning to work in the country: expert, investor, and labor, illustrating types of employment and projects. "Expert" is intended for foreigners employed by international as well as some non-government organizations; "investor" for investing funds in an enterprise (registered in Laos), but for this they require an investment license or proof of an enterprise registration: and finally "labor" for those "simply working" on a fixed employment contract, as regional or international workers. For the investor visa there is also a One-Stop Service (OSS), or "single window system."

Laos has been described as having "low administrative efficiency" and because of this many volunteers work without the proper visas, using tourist ones. This is risky, as the penalties can be significant.

BUSINESS RELATIONSHIPS

As elsewhere, developing a solid business relationship takes time and effort, and foreign businesses that have been successful in Laos have taken considerable time to build the necessary business and government contacts to operate successfully.

Social engagements such as formal dinners and, recently, even playing golf, are also useful ways to create a level of mutual trust and understanding between business partners. There is also a drinking tradition— the strong alcoholic *lao-lao* rice drink in olden times, foreign whiskeys today. The custom is that a host drinks first, in front of everyone present, and then walks around the room offering a shot glass of whiskey to each guest. A guest of honor can be offered this important role, but sometimes taking a drink in front of each guest might be required, which can be tricky!

Even though people in Laos are generally not direct in their everyday speech, face-to-face contact is very important in initial business encounters, as meeting a potential business partner in person allows for easier ongoing contact. It is, of course, best to avoid any confrontational or aggressive behavior.

INVESTMENT OPPORTUNITIES

Among the many potential business opportunities in Laos, the most popular ones for individual or SME investors seem to be related to tourism. More visitors are seeking the comfort of decent hotels and hostels, restaurants, cafés, shops, spas, guided tours, activity adventures, and so on. Foreign entrepreneurs and investors have experience of these industries. Others are looking for a new home and lifestyle with an income in this beautiful and underdeveloped country.

Tourism: Regional Domino Effect

Not only do Westerners want to travel to Laos, but there are more and more regional visitors. Asians flock from all over to enjoy a Laotian vacation, with Malaysian bikers driving north and many Chinese cars heading south from Kunming. Often, official groups of people travel together in convoys from Vietnam or China.

Global companies are focusing on the larger tourist and other projects to invest in the country's rapidly developing infrastructure. New roads, the railway, the dams, mining, and forestry call for huge contracts involving foreign expertise, meaning jobs for engineers, miners, consultants, and of course some jobs for the people of Laos. The former are extremely well paid, while the Laotians tend to be unskilled menial workers and laborers on low pay. With the gradual establishment of an education and training system in Laos, this will start to change.

FOREIGN AID AND DEVELOPMENT WORK

After the fall of the Soviet Union in the 1990s, Laos finally opened up to the outside world, revealing a country in dire economic straits, with most of its inhabitants suffering extreme poverty. Even now, and despite economic reforms, Laos relies heavily on foreign aid.

And this foreign aid is not without its difficulties. The developed world inevitably aspires to make developing countries become more like developed ones, but the sheer social, political, and cultural differences can make this very hard. There is often a combination of misunderstanding of intention, simple ignorance, and the inevitable greed and corruption. There are logistical and physical challenges in reaching communities in the rural areas, and the Sustainable Development Goals in the health and education sectors are proving difficult to achieve. Thus the rural population also engages in migrant laboring, receives remittances from relatives abroad, and undertakes multiple livelihood strategies.

Lao PDR is a resource-based economy, driven by forestry, agriculture, hydropower, and minerals, and it has been recently on a stable growth path. However, the distribution of such income is highly uneven, and also linked to problems in the day-to-day administrative management of the country.

Once the United Nations International Anti-Corruption Day started to be officially mentioned in Laos—with a ceremony held there in 2006—this was interpreted as a positive sign that at least discussing this extremely sensitive topic was feasible if conducted in a "diplomatic way." It was hoped that the ceremony demonstrated that there was an acceptable public space available for the discussion of issues considered politically sensitive, although some described it as an "encapsulation in a fanfare of empty rhetorical condemnations by high-ranking officials and foreign dignitaries ... while it should instead be debating with the use of practical examples." It has been suggested that investigating the financial basis and transparency of the ownership or use of each SUV Lao car would be an interesting point of departure, as these seemed mathematically impossible to afford in the light of public office salaries.

LAND OWNERSHIP

The legal situation is somewhat ambiguous. Section 17 of the Constitution states that all land in Laos is part of the national heritage. This is also stated in Section 3 of the Law on Land, according to which "land of the Lao PDR is under the ownership of the national community as prescribed in Article 17 of the Constitution." The Law on Land then spells out the rights and obligations of all Lao citizens concerning land, and in particular provides for a Laotian person to have "land use rights," which is the closest he or she can come to what Westerners would recognize as land "ownership." Some sections of the law cover the rights of foreigners regarding land, but in reality these are rights to leases or "concessions" on land, and do not equate to the "land use rights" accorded to Lao citizens.

If the land to which one has right of use is nationalized (or even ceded to someone else), specific laws rule that the state pays compensation to persons with "land use rights." However, the information regarding the evaluation and amount of compensation is far from clear. It appears to be conducted on case-by-case basis, and is unlikely to be compensation in full.

Many foreigners visiting Laos are tempted to stay, and some even consider starting a business or buying a home, not realizing that owning an apartment, house, or land here is not legally possible. They can secure long-term leases from Lao citizens or the state, or, strangely, buy an entire building but only lease the land it is on.

There are many other legal technicalities that need careful consideration. It is very difficult, if not impossible, to obtain Lao nationality; even Lao citizens who have been away from the country for more than seven years struggle to regain it. They, and foreigners marrying Lao partners, will secure nationality sooner than the average foreign applicant, but it should be borne in mind that foreigners must relinquish their original nationality and passport.

There is no such thing as a retirement visa in Laos. Because of this, many foreigners choose to buy property in one of the neighboring countries instead, and spend time in Laos on a regular tourist visa.

People tend to forget that Laos has almost been frozen in time, under a regime where nationalization is still a real possibility, and where favoritism is shown to politicians and the military. The influx of visitors and investors over the past few years is all so new to the country. However, Lao PDR is becoming increasingly aware of the need to promote business investment and to encourage and find ways for permanent residents to buy property, as all of this promotes further investment and employment for locals. They are particularly keen to enable foreign experts to stay in the country. The government is therefore looking into ways of regularizing these matters, and new "expert" visas are being put in place, but this will take time to effect.

Lao people are still buying land, despite the risk that it may be taken from them under a nationalization scheme and all they can expect is monetary compensation, often only minimal. They are also keen to lease it to foreigners for long-term use under a dubious "land use rights" agreement, whereby the foreigner may also be at risk and forced to relinquish it to the state. There are now many reputable law firms operating in Laos, and it is essential to consult one regarding any potential long-term use of land and property.

chapter nine

COMMUNICATING

LANGUAGE

Lao is the official national language in Laos, which, considering its modest size and population, has a remarkable linguistic diversity. Ironically, even if a foreigner makes every effort to learn the basics of Lao, he or she will still not find it easy to communicate with all the country's inhabitants. There are numerous ethnic languages, of which many people still speak only their own. The other insurmountable cultural barrier is the ongoing poverty and lack of education.

"Tai" vs "Thai"

Lao is described as a "Southwestern Tai language," and is spoken by approximately 25 million native speakers in Laos, Thailand, Cambodia, and Vietnam. Tai languages comprise a closely related linguistic family, of which the Thai language of Thailand is the most widely spoken member. The word "Tai" is used to refer to the entire group, because "Thai" is designated as the language of Thailand.

Lack of accurate data makes it difficult to confirm the number of languages spoken in Laos—research has been limited by problems of access—but there are an estimated eighty living languages and around 120 distinct dialects. Most of the minority languages are endangered, with a few exceptions (notably Hmong and Khmu). The strongest neighboring foreign languages heard and used in Laos are Thai, Vietnamese, and Mandarin. Children watch Thai TV, absorbing the language through cartoons and commercial jingles. There are still many Lao citizens who can't speak or write their national language, and it's not just smaller ethnic groups but large ones like the Hmong.

The Lao alphabet, or *akson Lao,* is the primary script used to write the Lao language and some other minority languages in Laos. It was also used to write the Isan language in Thailand, but it was replaced by the Thai script.

ສະບາຍດີ

Lao Literature

There is a surprisingly small number of books published in the Lao language, for both children and adults.

The rich oral tradition of poetry and folklore among the Lao predates their written literature and is still very much alive. The earliest evidence of written literature dates from the sixteenth century. In the nineteenth century the great social and political upheavals in the region became a prominent literary theme, often expressed in Buddhist and mystical terms. Lao literature was deeply influenced by the literary tradition of the neighboring kingdom of Lan Na in present-day Thailand.

Gradually, religious schooling was replaced by secular, government-sponsored education, and traditional Lao literature declined; it was also changing due to Thai and Western influence. Maha Sila Viravong was an important scholar of traditional Lao literature and history. His three children, Pakian Viravong (pseudonym Pa Nai), Duangdeuan Viravong (Dauk Ket), and Dara Viravong (Duang Champa), are well-known Lao writers from the mid-twentieth century.

LANGUAGE DYNAMICS TODAY

In today's world, where spoken national languages are reinforced with standardized spelling and grammar, the writing of Lao in Latin script is confusing. There is no standard system of transliteration and the result is a mix of English and French spellings. It doesn't help that the country itself is known as Laos as well as Lao PDR in many official "world countries" listings!

"Lao" vs "Laos"

The official name of the country is Lao PDR, and in the much-used alternative of Laos the "s" of Laos can either be pronounced or not. The various versions of its name—Laos, Lao PDR, and even Pathet Lao—are confusing. In French the "s" technically remains silent, although during colonial times it was they who added the letter to pluralize Lao as a noun for the people. Now they have followed other Europeans and do pronounce the "s"!

Only "Laos" or "Lao PDR" is used as the name of the country. "Lao" is not used as a noun to refer to the country; it can be an adjective, and a noun only when it refers to the people or language. Lao people do not pronounce the "s" when saying the name of their country, or certainly not when speaking Lao. They refer to it as "*Pathet Lao*," meaning "Lao Country."

It's worth noting that cultural groups in many Asian countries pronounce the name of their country differently. China, for example, has thirteen written languages—and not one of them pronounces "China" in the same phonetic way!

The Lao, the Lao People, the People of Laos ...

What is the best term? It is still a sensitive issue with such a diverse ethnic history and presence, and has long been debated by academics. Professor John Walsh calls the population "the Lao people." Technically this would refer only to the Lao, the major ethnic group, where "Laotian" might mean citizens of Laos as a whole. President Obama addressed them as "the people of Laos," indicating the entire population of a country striving to become a single nation. This will take time and, yes, the different people of Laos may gradually merge into one, but with the regrettable loss of some cherished ethnic identities and legacies along the way.

LEARNING LAO

So, how easy is it for a foreigner to pick up the Lao language? One thing is sure, and that is that the Lao will really appreciate your efforts to learn a few words of their language. Even if they are mispronounced, basic greetings or the odd phrase will go down well, and may even prove an icebreaker in initial business dealings. If you get it wrong, and see them laughing, no offense is meant. Your effort shows that you are eager to understand their culture.

Like Thai and Vietnamese, Lao is a tonal language—words are differentiated not only by the vowels and consonants but also by tone. There are five different tones in Lao: flat, high, low, rising, or falling. If pronounced incorrectly, the tone changes the meaning of the word entirely. Thus the three tonal options for the word *paa* have entirely different meanings—fish, jungle, and aunt!

You'll also need to get the hang of the alphabet, which has twenty-six consonants. Each consonant has a word associated with it to distinguish between a few sounds that have more than one letter, such as "s" and "h" which have two letters each. There are three "k" letters, a mixture of "k" and "g," in fact.

Another couple of points about the alphabet are that the letter "r," which was to be entirely eliminated in the old revolutionary system, is making a comeback, and that the sound of "ch" becomes "x," but is pronounced as an "s." So *xang* sounds like "sang," and means elephant! It's challenging, but worth the effort.

The Lao language is short on classic Western polite phrases. While "thank you" (*kop chai*) is widely used, the word for "please" (*karunaa, galuna, khaluna*) is very rare in everyday speech, and only really used in customer service recordings or when speaking to high-ranking government officials.

HUMOR

The people of Laos have a great sense of humor. The legendary trickster of Lao folklore, Xien Mieng (Xiangmiang), who constantly plays tricks on others and is not easily outwitted, is still hugely popular. He's a fun character dating back to the eighteenth century, since when stories have been transmitted by word of mouth or written on palm leaves. Oral history and folklore are strong traditions in Laos, and children are still in thrall to the ancient characters and taboos.

WAYS OF SAYING "YES"
Ko/go dai

It's worth knowing that you might easily confuse two basic Lao terms for "yes" and "no," which can often sound similar to the Western ear and cause problems in the market! "*Dai*" means possible, and "*ko/go dai*" means yes, while "*bo dai*" means no. When you've grasped a few words and can ask a question, it could be that you misunderstand the reply—is it "Yes, it's possible" (*ko/go dai*) or "No, it's not" (*bo dai*)?

The royal "*doi*" vs the proletarian "*cao/tchao/jao*"

Doi is the word for "yes" that was used before the Pathet Lao took over and "*cao*" became a norm. However, *doi* has now made a comeback, particularly in service industries, and one hears it a lot, even as a simple acknowledgement of someone following a conversation as they nod their head. There is a third, informal way of saying yes, which is impossible to write and sounds like a deep inhalation of air. *Doi, men leo* (maen leeo) is the most polite, complete answer for "Yes, it's true."

Royalty and the natural environment play a huge part in these stories.

There are many Lao proverbs and maxims. Here are two: *Khouam pha ya yarm you sai khouam sam let you thee nan*, (Where there's a will there's a way), and *Ya wai jai thang ya wang jai khon man ja jon jai to* (Don't believe people too much; it can land you in trouble!).

When it comes to jokes, acceptable topics can be quite different in Asia and the West. In Laos joking about weight is entirely acceptable; on the other hand, commenting on someone's dark complexion might be considered an insult. In fact, girls and women in Laos would find such a comment just as upsetting as someone in the West would if they were described as fat. There are also many jokes about names and nicknames, some totally incomprehensible to Westerners. If someone is called Keo, they may be greeted with "*Kin khao kap g/kuai bo*?" ("Did you eat rice with banana?") and everyone will laugh. It is apparently because of the way the same first letters sound.

OTHER LANGUAGES

The Lao are constantly exposed to Thai, Vietnamese, and Chinese, as these countries are all major providers of imported products, and of course TV programs. It is said that Lao is the archaic version of Thai, with Thai having more words for the same meaning. Written Lao is also the archaic form of written Thai, so it is much easier to write. According to one expert, Lao people find it easier to speak and read Thai, although often they cannot write it themselves. Thai people can barely understand Lao, don't like to try speaking it, and rarely read it, let alone write it.

Although French was widely used by the country's elite and in national education and administration (along with Vietnamese, after the monarchy was abolished and the Lao PDR took over) English is ever more present, especially with the Australian and American influence in Laos. In addition, the presence of other nationalities whose first foreign language is English makes it the only language that they can all communicate in, both among themselves and with the Lao population.

THE MEDIA

According to a National University of Singapore study, the Lao government owns all the country's newspapers and broadcast media. Khaosan Pathet Lao (KPL) is the official news agency, which supplies information to the other media institutions in compliance with government regulations, and publications must be approved by the Ministry of Information, Culture and Tourism.

Internet use and content in Laos involves a degree of online censorship. Conscious of their expected role, Lao officials also monitor local and international journalists covering politically sensitive topics. Official foreign employees have to follow specific rules that prohibit the online reading or downloading of potentially "controversial" Web sites on their work devices.

With law enforcement still being a bit of a gray area, international staff and consultants tread cautiously when it comes to exposing "sensitive topics." Even the media are reluctant to report "any illegal activity," as there is no media law defining the rights and responsibilities of journalists. "The law was not passed because the government does not think it is the right time," is a general thought often reported in the media. This will only change with time, and the emergence of a rules-based ethical journalism and reporting.

According to the BBC country profile, "In 2014, the government introduced strict new Internet controls, making online criticism of its policies or the ruling party a criminal offence. The new legislation also demands that Web users register with their real names when setting up social media accounts." Thus user accounts can be blocked if any article whose content can be interpreted as disrupting "social order" is posted on social media. Difficulties may arise if official government policies are not fully endorsed, as in the celebrated case of Swiss NGO Helvetas aid worker Anne-Sophie Gindroz.

Entertainment and News

Lao TV broadcasting is relatively new, so until now Thai radio and TV have played a huge role in Laos. Apart from cartoons for the kids (some American programs on the Lao government channels are dubbed into Lao), everyone enjoys Thai game shows and soaps (in the Thai language). Many people now view content and their favorite programs online.

Foreign-language radio stations are popular, the main ones being in English and French (Radio France Internationale, or RFI). Radio Australia sometimes has intermittent frequency.

CELL PHONES AND THE INTERNET

The country code for Laos is +856. Cellular phone services work well in all urban areas of Laos, although it does vary in rural locations.

It is advisable to buy a local SIM card, even if your international phone provider covers you for overseas, as local prices are often very competitive. In addition, the SIM card will cover all your Internet needs via the usual smart phone hotspot feature. You can buy Lao SIM cards easily and cheaply in many local shops, but you will need to register your personal details for security purposes before they are activated.

The main mobile telecom operators are Lao Telecom, ETL, Unitel, and Beeline, partly or fully owned by the Lao government. They all have different cover depending on the area, so if people are going somewhere remote, they tend to take two SIM cards with them.

The Impact of Cell Phone Technology

Before mobile technology took off in Laos, everyone relied on landlines. They're still used on a national basis, particularly in companies, where calls are technically free for workers, although there are sometimes restrictions on calls to cell phones.

Many people in Laos now have cell phones. They might have a cheap smart phone, an old hand-me-down, an ancient model, or a "copy" of a brand name phone, but, even so, for Laos, the development has been not unlike someone opening all the windows in a closed-up house. Locals thrive on their use, always tapping into free hotspots to save money. Some don't have the charger to their phone, and need to locate one. In rural areas, they might not even have the electricity for charging—but that doesn't stop them having cell phones!

It is not unusual to see monks speaking on their phones, and they doubtless download music and movie content just like anyone else. The combination of ancient religion and modern technology seems slightly bizarre and anachronistic, but communication is evidently important to everyone these days!

Globalization and new media trends have had a great impact on this country with such a small population among neighboring giants. Nevertheless, any activity on social media may be monitored.

MAIL

Snail mail! Receiving mail can prove to be a challenge in Laos, as there is no home delivery, and in any case most houses don't bear numbers or names. Most people arrange to receive mail at the Post Office by requesting a PO Box (where available); others use professional addresses if they have them, and some may request delivery at their consular services, particularly for important documents.

CONCLUSION

The peoples of Laos are an ethnic patchwork, whose rich and ancient cultures reflect their central geographical and historical position in Southeast Asia. Most of them are poor and live in deeply rural areas where daily life revolves around local and Buddhist customs and traditions, light years away from the official Marxism espoused by the government. Their traditional values of respect, deference to authority, social harmony, and the *boh pen nyang* philosophy of accepting and adapting to the situation served them well during the terrible years in which the Indochina wars affected every life.

Today this gentle, cheerful people have been catapulted into the modern era. People in Laos still speak softly and try to avoid confrontation, but there has been a shift away from reliance on advice and guidance from their elders and the religious hierarchy. Laos is now experiencing the social and economic impact of foreign enterprise and massive investment in tourism, rail links, mining, and hydropower. Together with the drive toward "national homogenization," these present a real challenge to its traditional values and way of life. The official Laos tourism slogan promotes the country with two words: "Simply Beautiful!" Don't wait too long.

Further Reading

Bouté, Vanina, and Vatthana Pholsena. *Changing Lives in Laos. Society, Politics and Culture in a Post-Socialist State.* Singapore: NUS Press, 2017.

Brier, Sam, and Phouphanomlack (Tee) Sangkhampone. *Lao Basics: an Introduction to the Lao Language.* Hong Kong; Periplus editions. 2010.

DeBuys, William. *The Last Unicorn. A Search for One of the Earth's Rarest Creatures.* New York: Little, Brown and Company, 2015.

Economic Research Institute for ASEAN and East Asia (ERIA). *Asean Rising: ASEAN and AEC Beyond 2015.* Jakarta, 2016. http://www.eria. org/ASEAN_RISING-ASEAN_and_AEC_Beyond_2015.pdf

Enfield, N. J., "Lao as a National Language," in Evans, G. (ed.), *Laos: Culture and Society* (pp. 258–90). Chiang Mai: Silkworm Books, 1999.

Fadiman, Anne. *The Spirit Catches You and You Fall Down.* Farrar, Straus and Giroux, 1998. A wonderful introduction to Hmong vs Western cultural dilemmas.

High, Holly. *Fields of Desire: Poverty and Policy in Laos.* Singapore: NUS Press Pte Ltd, 2014.

De Lavenère, Véronique. *Music of Laos.* Maison des Cultures du Monde, 2004.

DK Eyewitness Travel Guide: Cambodia and Laos. London: Dorling Kindersley, 2011.

Evans, Grant. *A Short History of Laos; The Land in Between.* Allen & Unwin, 2010.

Ivarsson, Soren. *Creating Laos: the Making of a Lao Space between Indochina and Siam, 1860–1945.* Nias Press, 2008.

Pholsena, Vatthana. *Post War Laos; The Politics of Culture, History and Identity.* Singapore, New York: Institute of Southeast Asian Studies, Cornell University Press, 2006.

Rough Guide to Laos. London: Rough Guides, 2012.

Southiseng, Nittana, and John Christopher Walsh. *Understanding the Health of Family Business in Laos.* Bangkok, School of Management Publications, 2010.

Stuart-Fox, Martin. *A History of Laos.* Cambridge University Press, 1997.

The United Nations. *Lao PDR: From Millennium Development Goals to Sustainable Development Goals: Laying the base for 2030.* The United Nations, 2017.

Warner, Roger. *Shooting at the Moon. The Story of America's Clandestine War in Laos.* South Royalton: Steerforth Press, 1996.

Foreigners Writing about Laos

In modern literature, the British crime writer Colin Cotterill's twelve books in the mystery series set around the character of Dr. Siri Paiboun, a French-trained physician who is the national coroner of Laos, remain popular. These books are set in the mid-1970s, and offer great insight into the country and its people. Highly recommended.

Penny Khounta, an American Peace Corps volunteer married to a Lao, shared her fascinating life and struggle in Laos in her 2017 publication of *Love Began in Laos: The Story of an Extraordinary Life*. It describes the culture shock experienced by a middle-class Westerner living in Laos before the Communist regime took over in 1975, and how she strove to love and support her French-educated husband when he fell from grace as a government official. The keen observation and insight into her seven years in Laos prior to the closing of its borders, followed by the contrast she encountered on her return in the twenty-first century, make for a very interesting read.

Useful Web Sites

www.britannica.com/place/Laos

http://databank.worldbank.org/data/Views/country=LAO

www.adb.org/countries/lao-pdr/main

Sources

Some sources of information may or not be accurate, as they are based on the many personal accounts of people I have met over the years in Laos and who were almost certainly unwittingly subject to propaganda.

Many academic articles have been analyzed in order to cover the cultural aspects of this beautiful but little-known country, and international data have been used when assessing the current humanitarian situation.

Such a concise book opens up many new questions. Limited space and constant change, however, allow only for a snapshot in time.

culture smart! laos

Index

culture smart! laos

Acknowledgments

I would like to gratefully acknowledge John Walsh, professor at the Shinawatra University, Thailand, who initiated my involvement in this project, as well as the many friends, colleagues, and academics in Laos and abroad who contributed so generously to this guide in response to my queries. These include Noussone, Anne-Katrin Tubbesing, Malisa, Penelope, Susanne Herrmann, MaeYer, Kathryn, Catherine, Hongmatsa, Elisabeth, Soulisack, Stephan, Gill Bathgate and John Roxborogh for their very prompt final proofreading, Zoe, Philippe Bachimon, and many others, as well as all the Interplast local and international teams.

I could not have written this book without the valuable collaboration of my great friend Chele Fox, an inspiring writer who spent many hours transcribing my viewpoint of a country that I and my family have grown to love. Thanks and gratitude to them for their patience and understanding too.